couscous in Morocco, stroll to Germany for a knockwurst, to France for quiche, or to the United Kingdom for bangers and mash (don't turn up your nose—it's delicious). In other words, the gastronomic opportunities at Walt Disney World are bountiful, with nearly 6,000 different dishes on its collective menu. From appetizer to dessert, and even a nightcap, we hope this fills the bill.

Bon appétit!

— Editor

HELPING HANDS

This book was made possible thanks to a tireless team of dedicated diners and behind-the-scenes support. Special, heartfelt thanks go to Heather Reed Guay and to Karen McClintock, who have done so much to ensure the accuracy of *Birnbaum's Official Walt Disney World Dining Guide.*

Kudos to Diane Hodges, copy editor extraordinaire. Thanks also to Jennifer Eastwood, Nisha Panchal, Clark Wakabayashi, and Michelle Olveira for their editorial support and production panache.

Any list of acknowledgments would be incomplete without mentioning our founding editor, Steve Birnbaum, who continues to be an inspiration for us all, as well as Alexandra Mayes Birnbaum, who is a guiding light and careful reader of every word.

RESERVATION TRACKER

After placing a call to 407-WDW-DINE (939-3463) to book meals for your upcoming vacation, jot the details and confirmation numbers on this page!

_____

_____

_____

_____

_____

_____

_____

_____

_____

_____

_____

_____

_____

_____

BIRNBAUM GUIDES

2013

WALT DISNEY World DINING GUIDE

Wendy Lefkon
EDITORIAL DIRECTOR

Jill Safro
EDITOR

Jessica Ward
ASSOCIATE EDITOR

THE **OFFICIAL** GUIDE

Lois Spritzer and Pam Brandon
CONTRIBUTING WRITERS

Alexandra Mayes Birnbaum
CONSULTING EDITOR

A COMPLETE INSIDER'S GUIDE TO DINING DISNEY STYLE

DISNEY EDITIONS

NEW YORK

For Steve Birnbaum, who merely made all of this possible.

Other 2013 Birnbaum's Official Disney Guides:

Disney Cruise Line
Disneyland
Walt Disney World
Walt Disney World For Kids
Walt Disney World Pocket Parks Guide

ISBN 978-1-4231-5226-2
V381-8386-5-12231

Printed in the United States of America

A Word From the Editor

I t has been said (and sung) that "it's a small world after all." It is not. In fact, Disney's world is so vast and has dining places so plentiful (there are hundreds of them) that picking the right spot to satisfy your group's diverse tastes can be a daunting experience.

It doesn't have to be. We assure you that whatever your palate prefers—simple or sublime, fast food or fine dining—it's being served up somewhere at Walt Disney World. Of course, finding (and reserving) the meal of your dreams can be a challenge. That's where this book comes in. If you're in search of a light snack or a filling lunch, a character breakfast or a champagne brunch—you'll find it described within these pages. You'll also discover rousing dinner shows, theme park favorites, quiet gems off the beaten path, and much more.

Given the popularity of many WDW eateries, booking a table in advance is nearly as important as selecting a venue. Our "WDW reservations" explanation will help you do just that.

Don't forget, you also need to be thinking about what you want to do later in the evening. Please, take your time, and when you're ready to strategize after-dinner entertainment, just flip to our Pubs and Lounges chapter. It delivers the scoop on Downtown Disney and the BoardWalk entertainment zones, as well as compelling spots in the parks and resorts.

Rest assured, a lot of time and calories have gone into the creation of the dining guide you're holding. This is not merely an alphabetical restaurant listing—there are telephone books for that. Our hardy band of editorial gourmands has visited each and every establishment and sampled the fare. If we love a place, you'll know. If we agree that an eatery isn't worth a rave, it won't get one. But our opinions are just that, opinions. The truth is, one reader may see a giant turkey leg as a meal fit for a king, while the same snack leaves another feeling decidedly less regal. We understand that. Our goal is to provide all readers with the information necessary to ensure a successful Disney dining experience.

Chapters in this book are organized by Walt Disney World's parks and resort hotels, with one section focused on eateries within the Downtown Disney entertainment district, another devoted to dinner shows, and one focused on pubs and lounges. We've also included two bonus chapters: the first describes the Disney Dining Plan, and the second reveals some of the most revered and requested recipes in WDW history.

Dining establishments are noted for location, food quality and variety, and ambience. Within each entry there is a price rating and a listing of the meals served. Signature dishes may be listed, but menus (and chefs) do change, so if the braised lamb shank is *the* reason you're headed for a certain restaurant, it's best to call ahead.

If a seven-course gourmet meal is a crucial part of your vacation happiness, you're in luck. If you'd rather enjoy breakfast with Mickey Mouse or have lunch in a castle, you won't be disappointed. It's also possible to dine on

Table of Contents

How to Book a WDW Table 9

Disney Dining Plan 13

Magic Kingdom 17

Epcot 33

Disney's Hollywood Studios ... 53

Disney's Animal Kingdom 63

Downtown Disney 69

WDW Resorts 79

Character Meals 103

WDW Dinner Shows 113

WDW Pubs and Lounges 117

WDW Recipes 131

Where to Find (Indexes) 139

A GUIDE TO THIS GUIDE

This book is a comprehensive guide, with details about each and every eatery on Walt Disney World property. Rather than present you with a book of epic proportions, we've labored to keep the project pocket-sized by combining concise descriptions with handy symbols. Each restaurant entry is preceded by a symbol that indicates whether the establishment is a fast-food spot or a table-service restaurant. We've also indicated whether or not said restaurant is a participant in the Disney Dining Plan (refer to page 13 for details). Here's a rundown of the symbols:

🏃 = Fast Food (aka quick service)

🍽 = Table Service

🎈 = Disney Dining Plan participant

B = Breakfast

L = Lunch

D = Dinner

S = Snack

$ = Under $15

$$ = $15–$36

$$$ = $36–$60

$$$$ = $60 and up

Prices are *estimates* based on an average adult dinner consisting of a soft drink, entrée, and either one appetizer, side order, or dessert *before* tax and tip. (Breakfast and lunch generally cost less.)

How to Book a WDW Table

The guide you are holding will help you select an ideal locale in which to enjoy every Walt Disney World meal. Picking the perfect place, however, is merely step one in the Disney dining experience. We cannot overemphasize the importance of the follow-up step: *booking* it—well in advance. For an explanation of WDW's unique reservations system, turn the page.

Walt Disney World Reservations

Walt Disney World has reservations about reservations. It seems the traditional system inevitably led to delays, thanks to no-shows and latecomers. As a means of expediting matters, Disney modified the process. Essentially, this means that you arrange to receive priority treatment when it comes to being seated at an agreed-upon time. Here's how it works: Call to request a time at a table-service eatery; arrive about 10 to 15 minutes before the assigned time and check in; receive the next available table that can accommodate your party. (There may be a wait involved.)

If an eatery accepts reservations, make them. Times can be secured up to 180 days ahead; 407-WDW-DINE (939-3463) or *http://disneyworld.disney.go.com/dining/*. Hours are 7 A.M. to 10 P.M. Many restaurants will accommodate walk-ins who are willing to wait—just don't arrive starving!

Disney resorts often have a phone in the lobby area that provides direct contact with the "Dine Line." Simply touch 55—the call is toll-free. From theme park pay phones, touch *88 (also toll-free). Otherwise, call 407-WDW-DINE.

Hot Tip

At press time, dining prices for "kids" covered guests ages 3 through 9. Most WDW table-service eateries have special menus just for little ones. Fast-food establishments offer special kid-friendly items, too.

For same-day arrangements in the Magic Kingdom, go to City Hall; in Epcot, head to Guest Relations; in Disney's Hollywood Studios, go to the corner of Hollywood and Sunset; in Animal Kingdom, ask at Guest Relations. Bookings can be made at Downtown Disney Guest Relations. Of course, plans can also be made at the restaurants themselves.

Keep in mind that a WDW restaurant reservation is not a traditional reservation. You may have to wait a while when you arrive at your assigned time. Rest assured, your party will be given the first table that opens up.

Note that WDW dinner shows (page 113) must be booked in advance. The Hoop-Dee-Doo Musical Revue, the Spirit of Aloha dinner show, and Mickey's Backyard Barbecue accept requests up to 180 days in advance.

Finally, the Disney dining scene is ever-evolving and procedures tend to change, so we advise calling 407-WDW-DINE to confirm current reservation policies.

NO RESERVATIONS? GOOD LUCK!

Disney's reservations system may allow for walk-ins (who are willing to wait). That said, the popularity of the Disney Dining Plan has made spontaneity something of a challenge. If you get caught without reservations during peak dining hours, consider eating earlier or later than the masses usually do. Here are a few of our favorite table-service places to pop into without an advance reservation (though there is usually a wait involved):

- Big River Grille & Brewing Works (BoardWalk)
- ESPN Club (BoardWalk)
- Hollywood Brown Derby (Disney's Hollywood Studios)
- House of Blues (Downtown Disney, West Side; 407-934-BLUE)
- Il Mulino New York Trattoria (Swan)
- Paradiso 37 (Downtown Disney, Pleasure Island)
- Portobello (Downtown Disney, Pleasure Island)
- Raglan Road (Downtown Disney, Pleasure Island)
- Yachtsman Steakhouse (Yacht Club)

Disney Dining Plan

To some, it may sound too good to be true: enjoy the convenience of pre-paid meals and stretch your vacation dollar by up to about 20–30 percent in the process. But the Disney Dining Plan is just that—a package "add-on" that lets guests redeem meal credits at more than 100 on-property eateries and, by doing so, actually save a few bucks. The plan is flexible, too. Feeling famished? Have an extra snack or a whole meal today and skip one tomorrow. Want to be waited on hand and foot all day? Throw caution to the wind and cash in three table-service meals. Of course, that means you'll have an abundance of quick-service experiences in your future, but who cares? You're on vacation. Do what makes you happy. To learn more about the Disney Dining Plan, turn the page.

The Dining Plan is available to any guest staying at any resort that's owned and operated by Walt Disney World. (That means all resorts on WDW property, with the exception of the Swan, Dolphin, Buena Vista Palace, Best Western Lake Buena Vista, Doubletree Guest Suites, Wyndham, Hilton, Holiday Inn, and Hotel Royal Plaza.) The plan, which starts at about $40 a day for adults, *must be purchased at the same time the resort is booked*. Together, the room and the dining plan are known as the Magic Your Way Plus Dining package. Here's what's included in the basic Dining Plan (there are also Deluxe, Quick Service, Premium, and Platinum packages):

- One "Table Service" meal (includes buffets) per person, per night of the package stay.
- One "Quick Service" meal per person, per night of the package.
- One snack per person, per night of stay.

In other words, if you are booked for 6 nights at, say, the Polynesian or any other Disney-owned-and-operated resort, you are entitled to 6 table-service meals, 6 quick-service meals, and 6 snacks during your stay.

One Table Service Meal includes an entrée, dessert (except at breakfast), and a non-alcoholic beverage, *or* one full buffet plus soft drink. One non-alcoholic specialty beverage may be substituted for dessert.

Hot Tip

Just because your meals are pre-paid, it doesn't mean they're pre-booked! Make reservations for table-service restaurants by calling 407-WDW-DINE (939-3463).

Hot Tip

One Quick Service Meal includes an entrée, dessert (dessert is for lunch and dinner only), and a non-alcoholic beverage, or one complete combo meal, plus one dessert (lunch and dinner), and a single serving of a soft drink.

One Snack consists of any of the following:
• Frozen ice cream novelty, ice pop, or fruit bar
• Popcorn scoop (single-serving box)
• Single piece of whole fruit
• Single-serving bag of snacks
• 20-ounce bottle of soda or water
• Medium fountain soft drink
• 12-ounce coffee, tea, or hot chocolate
• Single serving of pre-packaged milk
  or juice

When it comes time for a meal or a snack, be sure to present your hotel room key (aka your "key to the World" card) before ordering. That way your server will know to charge meals to your Disney Dining Plan. Tax is included, but gratuity is not. Please remember to tip your server!

Each time you redeem meals or snacks from the plan, your server or cashier will give you a receipt showing the remaining balance on your Dining Plan. For example, if your party of four started with 20 table-service meals and everyone in the group used one table-service meal, your receipt would indicate a balance of 16 table-service meals for the remainder of your stay.

DISNEY DINING PLAN

Hot Tip

A "quick-service only" Dining Plan is a cost-efficient option. It starts at about $20 per person, per day and includes 2 quick-service meals and 1 snack a day. Everyone on the plan gets a refillable mug.

Snack credits must be redeemed at participating Walt Disney World locations. In this book, we've indicated these establishments by placing a 🐭 by each restaurant. However, as specifics may change, we recommend visiting *www.disneyworld.com* or calling 407-939-3463 for updates.

Finally, be aware that unused meals expire at midnight on your package reservation check-out date. So, on the last day of your trip, eat like there's no tomorrow! Note that table-service items are meant to be consumed on-site. In other words, please don't request a giant doggie bag.

SIGNATURE RESTAURANTS

The following "Signature" restaurants, dinner shows, and character dining experiences require guests to redeem *two credits* when using the Disney Dining Plan: Jiko—The Cooking Place, Flying Fish Cafe, California Grill, Le Cellier, Hollywood Brown Derby, Hoop-Dee-Doo Musical Revue, Mickey's Backyard Barbecue, Cítricos, Narcoossee's, the Spirit of Aloha, Artist Point, Yachtsman Steakhouse, Cinderella's Royal Table, and private dining (room service).

Magic Kingdom

A lot has changed since Walt Disney World's original theme park opened in 1971. Back then, when it came to quelling hunger pangs, it was pretty much burger or bust. Nowadays, the options are a lot more diverse—with everything trom egg rolls to cinnamon rolls, smoked turkey legs to lamb stew, and clam chowder to seafood fra diavolo. Regardless of your tastes or budget, the six "lands" in the Magic Kingdom boast a bounty of palate-pleasers for the whole family.

ADVENTURELAND

✈️ Aloha Isle

S **$**

Switzerland meets Hawaii (hey, this *is* the Magic Kingdom) at this snack stand across from the Swiss Family Treehouse. Stop here for all things pineapple—juice, spears, floats, and the perennial favorite, the Dole Whip frozen pineapple soft-serve dessert. This spot has been around forever—they're definitely doing something right.

✈️ Sunshine Tree Terrace

S **$**

After you visit the singing birds in the Enchanted Tiki Room or fly on a magic carpet, you can take a cool break with some of the chilliest snacks in the park—citrus slushes (orange- or lemon-flavored). Cappuccino, iced cappuccino, a variety of soft-swirl ice cream floats (made with soda or iced coffee), espresso, and soft drinks round out the menu. A Walt Disney World staple, the Sunshine Tree has been dishing out treats to Magic Kingdom guests for as long as we can remember.

✈️ Tortuga Tavern

L **D S** **$-$$** ♥

This shady stop across from Pirates of the Caribbean invites you to munch on cheesy nachos, chicken or beef burritos, and taco salads. Kids can choose cheese quesadillas. Soft drinks are also served. The venue operates seasonally, so it may not be open during your visit.

FANTASYLAND

🍽 Cinderella's Royal Table

B L D **$$$** 🐭

You don't have to be a prince or a princess
to eat like one. At least, not here in the
Magic Kingdom. This regal establishment,
tucked inside Cinderella Castle, is a high-
ceilinged re-creation of a majestic mead
hall. It's small as Disney restaurants go, but
there's no feeling cramped—thanks to a lim-
ited number of tables and towering windows
that overlook Fantasyland. It's definitely the
most upscale eatery in this kingdom, but for
many, it's worth every royal penny.

Cinderella welcomes "Fairytale Dining"
guests into her home for three meals a day
and greets them in the castle lobby, while
her princess friends mingle in the dining
room. Dinner guests can feast on dishes
such as beef tenderloin, seafood pasta, and
stuffed chicken breast. Breakfast and lunch
fare tends to be upstaged by Cinderella and
friends. The *enormously* popular meals tend
to book up the full 180 days ahead, leaving
no room for spontaneity. (See page 21 for
details on booking.)

Breakfast costs about $43 for adults, $28
for kids ages 3 through 9. The price includes
the Princess Photo Package (see page 22).
Lunch costs about $46 for adults, $29 for
kids ages 3 through 9, including the Princess
Photo Package. In addition to a tableside visit
by Disney princesses, dinner includes an
appetizer, entrée, beverage, and dessert.
Dinner costs about $54 for adults, $33
for kids, and includes the photo package.
Reservations are a must. Call *exactly 180 days
in advance*, first thing in the morning (7 A.M.

Hot Tip

Fantasyland's expansion has brought with it a new full-service dining experience— the Be Our Guest restaurant inside Beast's Castle. Guests here may enjoy a meal in the library, west wing, or ball-room. Reservations are recommended.

Eastern Standard Time), and keep your fingers crossed. (Guests staying at a WDW resort should read the Hot Tip on page 11.)

Cheshire Cafe

S **$**

What's appealing about this snack shack is its ability to cool you off with a lemonade, lemon slush, juice, iced cappuccino, and other drinks. Cereal and muffins are served, too. On a path that borders Tomorrowland, it's easy to miss—so pay attention.

The Friar's Nook

L D S **$**

A trip to this window, located near Storybook Treats, can yield freshly made potato chips, hot dogs, chicken nuggets, soft drinks, and snacks such as carrot cake and apple caramel dippers. Operates seasonally.

Pinocchio Village Haus

L D S **$–$$** ❤

One of the better spots to target with kids in tow is Pinocchio Village Haus. It may seem small from the outside, but there are many dining rooms through that door. One room boasts picture windows that overlook the

TOUGHEST TiCKETS iN TOWN

Cinderella's Royal Table character dining is—hands down—the most difficult reservation to secure at Disney World. Why? For starters, Cinderella is one popular princess. And there's the allure of dining in the castle—the most famous landmark in the world's most popular theme park. Add to that the fact that the restaurant is small (122 seats) and you end up with a supply-and-demand issue.

The good news is, thanks to a change in policy and the addition of a princess-hosted lunch, it's gotten slightly less impossible to snag a seat at Cinderella's table. Potential guests still reserve by calling 407-WDW-DINE (939-3463) 180 days ahead, but now they must pay for the meal at the same time the reservation is booked. There is no charge for infants, but they must be included in the reservation.

Expect your credit card to be charged immediately upon making the reservation. Cancellations or changes must be made at least 24 hours prior to the reservation to receive a refund. The only one who can change or cancel a reservation is the one whose name is on the card.

Reservations cannot be transferred, and the lead name may not change.

Guests must present the credit card that was used to book the reservation, but may charge the meal to a different card or the Disney Dining Plan.

Continued on page 22

Continued from page 21

If your vacation package includes meals, you'll still have to make a reservation with a credit card. Make sure you tell the fine folks at WDW-DINE all about your package, including the confirmation number.

Finally, a word about the Photo Package: A cast member will snap a photo of your party with Cinderella inside the castle lobby. By the end of your meal, you'll receive a package including four 4-by-6-inch prints and one 6-by-8-inch print of your group, plus one 6-by-8-inch print of the castle. The Photo Package is included with the price of the meal.

Whew! That's a lot of work for one dining experience. Is it worth it? Judging by the smiles we see day in and day out, we have to say yes. Breaking bread in Cinderella's royal residence is, for many, a memory of a lifetime. (Just don't tell kids about the experience until you've secured a reservation!)

It's a Small World loading area. It's fun to watch the boats bob by as you munch on lunch. This is a good place to take kids (or picky eaters). Pinocchio offers pizza, meatball subs, chicken nuggets, salads (Caesar and Mediterranean), fries, chocolate cake, cheesecake, and soft drinks. Combo meals are offered. This is a popular destination in a busy neighborhood, so you may want to go a bit before or after traditional mealtime rush hours.

Hot Tip

The hours from 11 A.M. to 2 P.M., and again from about 5 P.M. to 7 P.M., are mealtime rush hours in the Magic Kingdom. Try to eat earlier or later whenever possible.

Storybook Treats

`S` `$`

Ice cream fans will appreciate this window near the Many Adventures of Winnie the Pooh. It offers soft-serve cones and cups, hot fudge sundaes and brownie sundaes, plus milk shakes and floats.

FRONTIERLAND

The Golden Oak Outpost

`L D S` `$`

Located on the outskirts of Frontierland, near the Adventureland border, this little wagon can satisfy big appetites. Stop here for fried chicken breast sandwiches, chicken B.L.T. flatbreads, veggie flatbreads, chicken nuggets, fries, triple chocolate cake, carrot cake, chocolate chip cookies, soft drinks, and more.

Pecos Bill Cafe

`L D S` `$–$$` 🟡

Pecos Bill—a classic "oldie but goody"— has been feeding hungry cowpokes for more than three decades. The look has changed a bit over time, but the reliable quality of the vittles remains. Cheeseburgers, sandwiches (such as barbecue pork), chili, chicken Caesar salads, chilled chicken wraps, and chili cheese fries are the staples. (If you'd rather skip the fries, ask for an à la carte version or an apple slice substitute.) Veggie burgers and strawberry yogurt round out the menu. Kids can choose from burgers, turkey sandwiches, or peanut butter and jelly sandwiches.

What sets this spot apart from other burger establishments? Two words: fixin's bar. It's full of items with which to garnish your meal. Among them: lettuce and tomato, and freshly sautéed mushrooms and onions.

The lines grow long during mealtimes. Resist the urge to jump on the first queue you hit and head toward a cashier that's farther from the entrance. The line may be shorter. Or better yet, take advantage of the Express Order station and skip the line altogether. (Technophobes, fear not: The kiosks are quite user-friendly.) Pecos Bill Cafe is one of the most popular eateries in the Magic Kingdom.

LIBERTY SQUARE

Columbia Harbour House
L D S $-$$

This lovely little spot adds some interesting (and healthy!) options to the quick service lineup, including fresh grilled salmon with couscous and steamed broccoli, lobster rolls, and the popular Lighthouse sandwich (with hummus, tomato, and broccoli slaw). You can still find fried shrimp, chicken nuggets, and clam chowder, too. For dessert there's strawberry yogurt and chocolate cake. Disney has done up this fast-food emporium with style—complete with antiques, model ships, harpoons, nautical

Hot Tip

To avoid lines, make a reservation at a Magic Kingdom restaurant that takes reservations—such as Be Our Guest, Tony's Town Square, Crystal Palace, or Cinderella's Royal Table. Know that you may have to wait a few minutes once you arrive at the eatery.

instruments, and even lace tieback curtains. In addition to the chowder, we savor the salmon and love that Lighthouse sandwich.

Liberty Tree Tavern
LD **$$–$$$** 🔴

Step back in time at this Early American tavern where the decor has had a tendency to outdazzle the fare. Here, the wallpaper looks as if it might have come from Colonial Williamsburg, the curtains hang from cloth loops, and the rooms are filled with mementos that might have been found in the homes of Thomas Jefferson, George Washington, and Ben Franklin. The restaurant is located across from the Hall of Presidents attraction.

The à la carte lunch menu includes salmon cakes, pot roast, turkey, salad, clam chowder, sandwiches, and soups. Dinner is an all-you-can-eat affair—salad, roast turkey breast, carved beef, smoked ham, mac and cheese, and more—served family style. The cost for dinner is about $32 for adults, $16 for kids ages 3 through 9. Dessert is included; specialty beverages are not. Despite the tavern motif, no alcohol is served (this kingdom is not only magic, it's dry). Reservations are recommended (try to arrive about 20 minutes early). Note that Disney characters do not visit here.

🏃 Sleepy Hollow

`S` `$`

Often missed by guests rushing toward the Haunted Mansion or other park hot spots, this window has a lot to offer: ice-cream cookie sandwiches, cookies, funnel cakes, Mickey-shaped waffles, and more are the sweets here. Also served? Coffee, hot cocoa, and other soft drinks. It's in the Hall of Presidents neighborhood near the Liberty Square bridge. Eat on the adjacent brick patio and get a view of Cinderella Castle at no extra charge.

MAIN STREET, U.S.A.

🏃 Casey's Corner

`L D S` `$` 🐭

Casey's is a grand slam for baseball fans—and those who just happen to love the food associated with America's pastime: big ol' hot dogs and salty fries. This old-fashioned

EARS TO YOU!

As if Mickey Mouse weren't already a sweet character, the folks at the Main Street Confectionery have made him even sweeter. Here you can get Mickey-shaped cookies, lollipops, crispie treats, candy-coated pretzels, and more. Elsewhere, you can snack on Mickey ice cream bars. They're easy to find and colossally popular. Guests gobble up more than three million of them each year.

red-and-white quick stop is on the west side of Main Street (adjacent to Crystal Palace). Tables spill out onto the sidewalk, where a ragtime pianist often tickles the ivories. There's a back room with a table or two, plus bleacher seating and constant screenings of sports-themed animated shorts. The bill of fare retains the mood—jumbo hot dogs (on huge rolls), corn dog nuggets, nachos, fries, brownies, cotton candy, and soft drinks. You gotta love a place that supplies free cheese sauce and malt vinegar for your fries. It's a popular spot for a late-night snack, and a Magic Kingdom classic.

Crystal Palace
B L D **$$–$$$**

A landmark of sorts, this restaurant—one of the prettiest in the Magic Kingdom—could be a Victorian garden if not for the walls and ceiling. The airy atmosphere provides a pleasant escape from the crowds on Main Street, and the all-you-can-eat buffet is a bountiful—if not terribly noteworthy— spread. Its main attraction is its character, make that *characters*: Winnie the Pooh and friends mingle with guests all day long.

Breakfast features a variety of hot and cold items, including omelets, fresh fruits, cereals, and such. The midday meal features a salad bar, deli bar, pasta dishes, chicken, and fish. Dinner offers more of the same: chicken, pastas, fish, carved meats, and more. Kids love the ice-cream sundae bar (lunch and dinner), as well as the pint-size and kid-palate-appropriate part of the buffet.

Located toward the end of Main Street, U.S.A. (near Adventureland), the "palace" takes its architectural cues from structures that once stood in New York and London's

Hyde Park, and from San Francisco's Conservatory of Flowers in Golden Gate Park. There's a Victorian-style indoor flower garden, with tables that look out on flower beds, while topiaries—Pooh, Tigger, Eeyore, and Piglet—greet guests at the entrance.

Cost for breakfast is about $23 for adults, $13 for children ages 3 through 9; lunch is about $25 for adults, $14 for children; dinner is about $37 for adults, $18 for children. Prices are higher during select "peak" seasons. Reservations are recommended.

Main Street Bakery

B L D S $ 🐭

Ever popular and always crowded, this old-fashioned bakery gives off a heavenly aroma and delivers with pastries, pies, sandwiches, and cookies. It's possible to get a quick breakfast, here, too—from bagels and breakfast sandwiches to warm cinnamon rolls. The built-to-order ice-cream cookie sandwiches and the chocolate-chunk cookies are popular indulgences. You can also get low-fat milk and soy milk, yogurt, fresh fruit, granola and other cereal—that is, if your willpower holds out.

Plaza Ice Cream Parlor

S $

This happy place for ice-cream lovers boasts the Kingdom's largest variety of hand-scooped ice-cream flavors, including no-sugar-added varieties. It's great for a before-the-parade or on-the-way-out-of-the-park nosh. To keep things moving, choose flavors and desired number of scoops before jumping in line. They have sundaes and floats, too.

 Plaza Restaurant

L D S | **$$** | 🐭

Not to be confused with the Plaza Ice Cream Parlor, this place also boasts ice cream as the specialty of the house. Oh, wait, that *is* confusing. Here's how to differentiate: The Ice Cream Parlor is a counter-service, cones-and-cups-only establishment. The Plaza is a table-service, you-name-a-way-to-serve-ice-cream-and-they-just-might-do-it establishment. Expect heaping sundaes, milk shakes, ice cream floats, and more. Hot and cold sandwiches (including tuna salad, fresh mozzarella, and Reuben sandwiches), salads, and hamburgers are also available, as is no-sugar-added ice cream.

The charming atmosphere and the quality fare combine for a sweet dining experience. Reservations are recommended.

Tony's Town Square

L D | **$$$** | 🐭

Here it's possible to savor a fine view of Town Square while you bite into Italian

Hot Tip

Is the Magic Kingdom open late today? If so, consider heading over to the Contemporary, Polynesian, Grand Floridian, or Wilderness Lodge to have an early dinner, and then return to finish the day at the Magic Kingdom. Remember to keep your ticket handy for re-entry to the park. Transportation (monorail and water taxi) generally runs for at least one hour after the park's posted closing time for the day.

SPECIAL REQUESTS

Watching your salt intake? Find lactose intolerable? Most of Disney's table-service restaurants can accommodate special requirements (such as allergies to gluten or wheat, shellfish, peanuts, etc.) if requests are made at least 72 hours in advance. It's best to make your needs known when you make your advance reservations (407-WDW-DINE). Confirm your reservation and special request before arrival. Guests requiring kosher meals are encouraged to make their requests when they make their reservations. Kosher meals must be reserved at least 24 hours ahead and require a credit card (the card will not be charged unless the reservation is canceled less than 24 hours prior).
Note: A 48-hour notice is needed for some table-service eateries. Kosher meals are not offered at Garden View Afternoon Tea, Teppan Edo, and Tokyo Dining.

specialties—pizzas, Caesar salad, sandwiches, and pasta. At dinnertime, Tony's menu offers chicken dishes, grilled steaks, and spaghetti, along with daily specials. (If you require gluten-free pasta, just ask—Tony is happy to accommodate.) Top it off with an Italian sweet and perhaps a foamy cappuccino.

If you time it right, you can fold your napkin, pay the check, and wander onto Main Street to enjoy the fireworks from one of the best vantage points in the Magic Kingdom. Reservations are highly recommended—especially during peak times of year.

TOMORROWLAND

Auntie Gravity's Galactic Goodies

`S` `$`

Ice cream may not seem futuristic, but chances are it'll be around at least another billion years, give or take. Located across from the Tomorrowland Speedway, Auntie G's offers up smoothies (strawberry-banana, orange-pineapple, and more), soft-serve ice cream, sundaes, and floats. Soft drinks are available, too. There's virtually no atmosphere in this corner of the galaxy, but we still gravitate toward the goodies.

TALKIN' TURKEY

Smoked turkey legs, that is. There's something barbarically compelling about gnawing on one of these popular mega-snacks. If you've had one, you know they're pretty good. Here are some things you may not know about these giant, high-calorie treats:

- Each one weighs about 1½ pounds.
- Disney guests gobble up more than 1½ million of them every year.
- The turkeys that once belonged to these legs weighed 40 to 50 pounds.
- They can be purchased at a cart in the Magic Kingdom's Frontierland and at the Lunching Pad at Rockettower Plaza in Tomorrowland.
- They cost about $9 a pop.

Cosmic Ray's Starlight Cafe

L D S | **$-$$** | 🐭

As big as all outdoors (not necessarily a plus), this is the largest fast-food spot in the park. Located across from Tomorrowland Speedway, it's like several fast-food spots in one. There are separate stations, with a different menu offered at each.

The variety is good, but you need to wait in more than one line if you want food from two or three sections. Choose from Bay 1 for rotisserie chicken, barbecue ribs, and chicken sandwiches; Bay 2 for cheeseburgers, vegetarian burgers, and hot dogs; and Bay 3 for soups, salads, sandwiches, and wraps. An Audio-Animatronics (Sunny Eclipse) lounge singer performs throughout the day.

Note: Cosmic Ray's Starlight Cafe offers a few kosher menu selections, too.

Lunching Pad at Rockettower Plaza

S | **$-$$** | 🐭

If it's just a snack you're after, stop at the base of the Astro Orbiter for sweet, cream-cheese-stuffed pretzels, frozen soda slushes, plain and chocolate milk (regular and soy)—and large "gourmet" hot dogs: Choose Philly cheesesteak, taco, or Coney Island dogs.

Tomorrowland Terrace

L D S | **$-$$** | 🐭

Near the Plaza Restaurant, this spot serves light fare such as burgers, lobster rolls, and salads. Tables near the water afford an impressive view of a topiary serpent and Cinderella Castle. This venue operates seasonally and may not be open during your visit.

Epcot

The eclectic, international lineup of fare offered here threatens to overshadow the attractions themselves. With no fewer than 11 different countries represented in the World Showcase section of the park, Epcot provides guests with the opportunity to eat their way around the world without leaving Central Florida. Less ambitious diners will likely have their taste needs met, too—there's a bountiful food court in Epcot's Future World, as well as a smattering of simple yet satiating snack spots.

FUTURE WORLD

EPCOT

Coral Reef (The Seas)

L D **$$$** ♥

This water-themed restaurant is all about nibbling on creatively prepared fish under the watchful eyes of their brethren. The restaurant is decorated in cool greens and blues to complement its surroundings, and every table has a panoramic view of a living coral reef; some are right up against the glass. (Don't worry: You're not actually eating Epcot residents—Disney's catches all come fresh from fishing boats in the Atlantic each day.) Menu items run the gamut from a bounty of fresh fish and shellfish, including shrimp, mahi mahi, and salmon—prepared in a number of ways—to grilled New York strip steak and pan-seared chicken breast for those who are satisfied by simply spying on fish. And save room for the "chocolate wave" dessert. Reservations are recommended.

Electric Umbrella (Innoventions Plaza)

L D S **$–$$** ♥

This large locale is decorated in shades of blue and magenta. The restaurant is a good bet when the weather is temperate enough to allow dining at the tables on the terrace outside—or when bound for World Showcase with finicky eaters in tow. (There are indoor tables, too.) Offerings include burgers, chicken breast nuggets, tossed salads, and assorted sandwiches. Soft drinks and desserts are also available. Kids tend to enjoy the fare here.

HOLIDAY HOOPLA

During the Christmas holiday season, Epcot's World Showcase hosts a special Candlelight Processional. The show features a stirring choral concert and a reading of the Nativity Story by a celebrity narrator. The event is free (with park admission), but the general admission seating fills up as early as two hours before showtime. Rather than wait in line, we prefer to book a dining package—one that combines lunch or dinner at a World Showcase restaurant with guaranteed seating at the Processional and fireworks viewing. For information, call 407-WDW-DINE. We highly recommend this package— sure, it's a luxury, but consider it an early Christmas present for yourself!

Garden Grill (The Land)
D **$$–$$$**

Guests are often so distracted by the sights and the jovial hosts (Chip, Dale, and friends) that they don't realize the restaurant is actually moving. As the restaurant revolves, and it does so quite slowly, tables drift past various dioramic scenes (which are part of the attraction Living with the Land). Among the nature scenes that may be served with dinner are a thunderstorm, sandstorm, prairie, or rainforest. The scenes were designed with diners in mind and provide you with a peek into a farmhouse window that's out of viewing range of the waterborne passengers.

Chip and Dale (who may be joined by Mickey Mouse and Pluto) host the character meal here each day. The menu features turkey breast, flank steak, seasonal fish, fresh vegetables (some of which are grown inside The Land pavilion), and a small selection of desserts. There is a separate kids' menu. For adults, the cost is about $35. Kids pay $17. Beverages and dessert (fresh-baked fruit crisp) are included. Meals are served family style (unlimited, communal platters for the table). Reservations are recommended. Prices may be higher during "peak" seasons.

The restaurant moves in a circle. It's imperceptible to most, but if you are highly sensitive to motion it may be best to dine in a more stationary environment.

Sunshine Seasons (The Land)

B L D S $–$$

It's the closest thing to a mall food court you'll find in a Walt Disney World park, but more upscale. Located near the entrance to Soarin' on the pavilion's lower level, this is an ideal destination for parties who can't quite agree on any one type of fare—there's bound to be something for everyone. Tables are scattered in several areas, beneath colorful hot-air balloons. Scouting out a table can be a challenge during peak mealtimes. (There can be quite a bit of pedestrian congestion, thanks to the enormous popularity of the Soarin' attraction.)

The Sandwich Shop offers a variety of sandwiches, including a Reuben panini, and an oak-grilled vegetable flatbread. **The Bakery**'s desserts include chocolate mousse cake, brownies, and ice cream bars. There is also a "grab and go" section for guests in a

DID YOU KNOW?

More than 30 tons of fruits and vegetables have been grown at The Land pavilion in Epcot and served to guests dining in Walt Disney World restaurants.

EPCOT

hurry. Among the items to choose from are sushi, fruit and cheese plates, salads, and snack foods. **Grill Shop** offers rotisserie chicken, grilled fish, and slow-roasted pork. **The Soup & Salad Shop** serves the likes of roasted-beet and goat cheese salads and seared-tuna salad with sesame rice wine dressing. There is a selection of soups, too. Finally, the **Wok Shop** has Mongolian beef with jasmine rice and noodle bowls (including one of the vegetarian variety).

A word of advice: It's a good idea to split up your party and stand in several lines at once. That'll increase your chances of actually eating together. Before you do so, select a table. That way, everyone in the party will know where to meet after they forage for their meals.

Hot Tip

That gift card burning a hole in your pocket? Disney Gift Cards may be redeemed at all Disney-owned-and-operated dining, shopping, and recreation locations where credit cards are accepted. If you lose track of what's left on your card, simply call the number on the back to find out.

WORLD SHOWCASE

📣 Akershus Royal Banquet Hall (Norway)

B L D | **$$–$$$** | 🐭

At Epcot's castle-like Akershus, guests are treated to authentic Norwegian cuisine. This is your chance to sample well-prepared signature dishes that rarely make their way into theme parks. Try a sampling of the Norwegian *koldtbord*, a buffet featuring smoked salmon and seafood, authentic Norwegian cheeses, and chilled salads, followed by one of the ever-changing line-ups of Norwegian-inspired entrées, including seafood, beef, and poultry selections. The kids' menu offers grilled chicken, ravioli, turkey and cheese roll-ups, and hot dogs. Dessert is included, as are soft drinks. Don't be daunted by the strange names of some dishes; servers will explain the offerings.

Princess Storybook dining takes place here daily (breakfast, lunch, and dinner). It's an excellent alternative to Cinderella's Royal Table (which is very difficult to reserve). While guests enjoy the all-you-can-eat fare, Disney princesses wander about and mingle. Belle, Jasmine, Snow White, Sleeping Beauty, and even Mulan have made appearances. Guests get a special souvenir at meal's end—a complimentary set of photos with one of the Disney princesses. (Each set includes one 6-by-8-inch print and four 4-by-6-inch prints and is presented in a themed folder.) Note that the character appearance schedule varies. Reservations must be made with a credit card. Changes and cancellations must be made at least 48 hours ahead to avoid a $10 per person charge.

 Biergarten (Germany)

L D **$$–$$$** 🐭

Year in and year out, this place makes us happy. It's a reasonably priced, all-you-can-eat buffet of traditional German cuisine set in a charming courtyard. Adding to the fun are communal tables and live entertainment (at lunch and dinner). It's pretty much Oktoberfest year-round.

The hearty, varied buffet features a selection of sausages, rotisserie chicken, spaetzle, chicken schnitzel, potato salad, cucumber salad, and many other German specialties. Wash it all down with soft drinks, German wine, or a stein of beer (suds purists may grouse at the limited selection of beer). Among the dessert options is apple strudel with vanilla sauce.

The entertainment consists of occasional appearances by traditional Bavarian musicians—each clad in lederhosen or dirndl—who play accordions, cowbells, a musical saw, and a harp-like stringed instrument known as the "wooden laughter." Performances take place at scheduled times in the dining room. Diners are usually invited to join the fun on the dance floor. Because entertainment is intermittent, there's plenty of time to enjoy the pleasant setting. Reservations are recommended, particularly during peak seasons.

Bistro de Paris (France)

D **$$$$**

This intimate bistro—one flight above Chefs de France—puts on romantic airs rather than the usual bustle. The elegant decor, with its evocative interplay of brass sconces, milk-glass chandeliers, mirrors, and leaded glass, is convincingly French. And, if you're one of the lucky few who arrive as a window-side table opens up, you'll be treated to a rather unique view of World Showcase.

The traditional upscale bistro menu (crafted by the same chefs responsible for the menu at Chefs de France; see page 41) features such robust "preludes" as escargot cassoulet or baby greens with warm goat cheese. The entrée menu includes a roasted duck breast, beef tenderloin, and Maine lobster risotto. This is hearty dining, so you might want to stroll around the promenade to walk off your meal—and your dessert soufflé. The wine list is *très* French. Reservations are recommended.

Boulangerie Patisserie (France)

L D S **$-$$** ❤

For some, a visit to Epcot is incomplete without stopping by this ever-popular (and newly expanded) pastry shop, tucked toward the back of the France pavilion. Crowds are forever lining up to consume the flaky croissants, éclairs, fruit tarts, and chocolate mousse. It's also possible to indulge in a

---

ONE-STOP SWEET SHOP

A delectable addition to the World Showcase landscape, the Germany pavilion's Karamell-Küche is sure to satisfy your sweet tooth—provided that you're a fan of fresh, gooey caramel draped or drizzled over chocolate, cookies, crunchy apples, and much, much more.

---

cheese plate, a ham and cheese quiche, or a ham and cheese croissant. The baguettes are *magnifique*. Wash it all down with espresso, cappuccino, or hot chocolate.

The treats were selected under the management of the chefs who were the culinary brains behind the Chefs de France restaurant not far away. This has become a favorite snacking stop among Epcot veterans. Your best bet is to stop here as soon as World Showcase opens or during IllumiNations, the nightly fireworks show (though you can't see the show from here).

Chefs de France (France)
L D **$$$–$$$$** ♥

"Bright lights, big dining room" describes this airy establishment. With some of France's best chefs responsible for this nouvelle French kitchen, the results are rewarding. The menu features fresh ingredients readily available from Florida purveyors, though the restaurant imports as many key ingredients from France as possible.

The offerings are French, but the foundation of the menu is nouvelle cuisine, which involves lighter sauces using less cream and butter than in classic French cooking. Menu items include broiled salmon, grilled beef tenderloin, and roasted duck breast. Soups and appetizers, such as onion soup and escargot, are all-day staples. Crème brûlée and chocolate profiteroles (cream puffs) are dessert favorites. Wine pairings are recommended from a well-rounded list.

Chefs de France is one of the most expensive World Showcase eateries. Still, given its perennial popularity, many guests agree it's worth the splurge. Reservations are a must.

🏃 Cool Post
(between Germany and China)

`S` `$`

As its name suggests, this place specializes in all things cool: ice cream, beer, and soft drinks—plus hot dogs. Located between the Germany and China pavilions, it may offer a refreshing spritz of water when the weather is warm.

🏃 Katsura Grill (Japan)

`B` `D S` `$` 🐭

Easy to miss, what with its out-of-the-way location, Katsura is an ideal spot to go to escape the masses and savor a simple, relaxing meal. The eatery (formerly known as Yakitori House) sits beside a small, peaceful garden. The fare here includes Asian flavors from sushi to Japanese curry, teriyaki and udon noodles, *edamame*, ramen noodle salad, and *okonomiuaki* (a Japanese pancake made with vegetables and topped with a tangy sauce). Drinks extend to green tea, Kirin beer, and sake.

🏃 Kringla Bakeri og Kafe
(Norway)

`B` `D S` `$–$$` 🐭

This bake shop serves *kringles,* sweet pretzels reserved for special occasions in Norway; cloudberry horns, flaky pastries filled with cream and cloudberries; *lefse* (potato bread with cinnamon sugar); and sandwiches such as open-faced smoked salmon and boiled egg slices, roast beef, and ham and apple. There are no seats in the bakery, but guests may eat in a shaded outdoor area.

🏃 La Cantina de San Angel (Mexico)

L D S **$–$$** 🐭

Located directly across from Mexico's pyramid, this lagoonside eatery serves traditional Mexican fare. Expect selections such as cheese empanadas, fresh guacamole and tortilla chips, nachos heaped with toppings, and beef or chicken tacos, plus caramel churros and frozen fruit pops. This is a prime spot from which to view the evening's presentation of IllumiNations. Beer and margaritas are available, as are soft drinks.

FOOD AND WINE FESTIVAL

Once a year, Epcot's hopping dining scene expands exponentially in what's known as the International Food and Wine Festival. The event, which usually runs from late September through early November, is a celebration of the flavors of dozens of nations. Those countries without permanent stations at World Showcase set up temporary displays from which authentic samples of food and wine are sold. The samples range in price from about $3 to $8. It's possible to eat and drink your way around the world for about the same price as some table-service restaurants.

The festival also features demonstrations from top chefs, as well as wine and cooking seminars. For specifics, visit www.disneyworld.com or call 407-824-4321. Make reservations as early as you can—this is one popular festival.

🍽 La Hacienda de San Angel (Mexico)

L D | $$–$$$ | 🐭

The Mexico pavilion's newest eatery, La Hacienda has a striking exterior that was designed to look like a south-of-the-border home. The attention to detail continues inside, with original artwork and lighting fixtures, and chairs and tables that were crafted in Mexico.

Most tables have a view of the lagoon, but seats near the windows double as front row seats for the evening's presentation of IllumiNations—Reflections of Earth. The dining room is a hot ticket for the nightly show, with music pumped inside.

Appetizers include warm chips and two salsas (one mild, one with zing), mini-tacos, black bean soup, and roasted sweet peppers with lime and sea salt, served with mini chorizo sausages. There are two entrées—one beef, one seafood—that are meant for sharing (though you may not want to). Flank steak or shrimp tacos, pork, chicken, and grilled tilapia dishes round out the menu. Reservations are recommended.

🍽 Le Cellier Steakhouse (Canada)

L D | $$–$$$ | 🐭

We love retreating to this peaceful wine-cellar-like spot, a favorite place for a hearty meal. The restaurant has low ceilings, lantern light, and stone walls, all of which contribute to the atmosphere.

There's a full menu of tempting Canadian foods, starting with a bread basket that includes a pretzel, plus sourdough, and whole-grain creations. At both lunch and dinner, the

B *breakfast* **L** *lunch* **D** *dinner* **S** *snacks*

cheddar cheese soup is a hit (it's been on the menu since Le Cellier opened). Midday, there's a steak salad or prime rib sandwich. Specialties such as pan-seared salmon and filet mignon are on both the lunch and dinner menus, along with pasta and pork dishes. For dessert, try the crème brûlée or chocolate cake. Canadian beers and wines are served. Disney Dining Plan participants should note that this eatery now boasts "Signature" status for dinner hours. Reservations are a must— this is a popular and relatively tiny restaurant.

Liberty Inn (The American Adventure)
L D S **$–$$**

While it may seem like the flavors of the United States get short shrift when it comes to representation at Epcot, that's not the case here. True, there's no America-oriented table-service restaurant at World Showcase, though the Garden Grill over in Future World proudly serves up platters of Americana. On the inter-national side of the park, Liberty Inn dishes out what many think of as American food: burgers, hot dogs, and fries. Also on the menu are (yummy) black bean vegetable burgers, chicken nuggets, salads, sandwich-es, and desserts (think baked apple blossom or a brownie). This is a good choice for children and picky eaters.

Lotus Blossom Cafe (China)
L D S **$–$$**

The fare may not live up to the splendor of the rest of this pavilion, but if you crave a quick Chinese food fix, this place, adjacent to the shopping gallery in the China pavilion, offers orange chicken, beef noodle soup bowl, salad, egg rolls, pot stickers, shrimp fried rice, and more. There is a covered outdoor seating area nearby.

🍽 Marrakesh (Morocco)
L D S $$–$$$ 🎯

It's not every day that you can slip into an exquisitely tiled Moroccan palace and be entertained by belly dancers and musicians as you polish off a plate of Moroccan cuisine; even the waiters are dressed in traditional costumes. Want to know how authentic this place is? The king of Morocco sent craftspeople to Epcot to make sure they were creating a real Moroccan atmosphere. (Unfortunately, the fare plays second fiddle to the surroundings.) The menu includes roast lamb, chicken brochette, beef shish kebab, and couscous. Sampler platters are available. Reservations are recommended, but it's often possible to get in without much of a wait.

🍽 Mitsukoshi (Japan)
L D $$$ 🎯

Within the sprawling Mitsukoshi complex (which is run by the Japanese company of the same name), there are two options:

Tokyo Dining fills a chic, colorful space in the Mitsukoshi building. If you're in the mood for sushi, sashimi, tempura, grilled chicken, salmon, or filet mignon, head here. For something unusual, try the grilled freshwater eel or braised pork belly slowly cooked in sake. It's possible to munch on *edamame* and indulge in sake and Japanese beer, among other drinks. A few window-side tables allow a view of the nightly presentation of IllumiNations. Reservations are recommended.

Teppan Edo, Tokyo Dining's lively neighbor, fills the space formerly occupied by Teppanyaki Dining Room. As with its predecessor, guests here sit around a large *teppan* grill and watch as a nimble chef demonstrates just how quickly enough chicken, beef, seafood, and vegetables to feed eight people can be chopped, seasoned, and stir-fried. Teppan Edo entrées are sizzling and satisfying. Soups, salads, sushi, desserts, and cocktails (including Japanese beer and sake) are also on the menu. Don't wear your finest attire: There's always the potential for a little splattering here and there. Reservations are recommended.

Nine Dragons (China)
LD $$$ 🐭

This stop on Epcot's varied international restaurant tour offers family-style meals prepared in provincial Chinese cooking styles. On the appetizer menu, expect to find items such as lightly spiced cucumber salad, shrimp summer rolls, and chicken dumplings. Entrées include everything from sweet-and-sour pork to the spicy kung pao chicken, vegetable stir-fry, five-spiced fish, and a peppery shrimp with spinach noodles.

A nice variety of imported Chinese teas, beers, and wines is available. Dessert selections include red-bean ice cream, ginger ice cream, and the house-baked ginger tiramisu. Reservations are recommended.

Refreshment Port (Canada)
S $

Located near Canada, this stand offers smoothies, chicken sandwiches, fried shrimp, fries, soft drinks, and soft-serve ice cream. It's a good spot for a quick snack.

Rose & Crown Pub & Dining Room (United Kingdom)
L D S **$$–$$$** ✿

Don't let the word "pub" throw you. While this place serves up some of the best brews on Disney property, its dining area is also known for such crowd-pleasing dishes as crispy fish and chips and bangers and mash (sausages with mashed potatoes).

Dessert options include sticky toffee pudding and Scotch whiskey cake. Bass ale from England and Harp lager and Guinness stout, both from Ireland, are on tap.

The pub section of the Rose & Crown serves such snacks as a U.K. cheese plate and fish and chips—along with all the brews noted above and traditional British mixed drinks. This spot is quite popular, so it's often necessary to queue up at the door. But the wait is seldom very long, since few guests choose to linger over their drinks. A piano player is sometimes on hand to entertain revelers. The pub section also spills out onto the promenade—where the first-come, first-snagged waterside tables make for a nice spot to sip a drink and/or enjoy a snack from a nearby stand. Reservations are not available in the pub areas, but are recommended for the restaurant.

San Angel Inn (Mexico)
L D **$$$** ✿

The lights are low, the mood is romantic, and there is a smoking volcano tableside. If that's not enchantment enough, there's also a moonlit river. It all takes place inside the pyramid that serves as the Mexico pavilion.

The recently revamped menu? You'll find

B *breakfast* **L** *lunch* **D** *dinner* **S** *snacks*

Mexican fare from margaritas to tempting tacos and enchiladas. And there's more: The eatery offers a variety of fish, poultry, and meat dishes. To start, there's *tlacoyos de chilorio* (corn cakes topped with refried beans, pork, cheese, sour cream, and green tomatillo sauce) and *tacos de filete* (grilled beef tenderloin served on a soft flour tortilla with chipotle pepper sauce, scallions, and avocados). Entrée selections include pan-seared tilapia; *carne asada a la Tampiqueña* (grilled tenderloin with cheese enchilada, black refried beans, red bell pepper, onion, rice, and guacamole); and pork tenderloin with a sauce of pumpkin, chiles, and almonds; plus soup and Caesar salads.

The desserts may be unfamiliar to diners, but are worth trying. The *crepas de cajeta* (warm crepes with caramel sauce and toasted almonds) are among the more popular treats. Beer and margaritas make good accompaniments. Reservations are recommended.

Sommerfest (Germany)
L D S **$-$$** ❤

Here, speedy sustenance takes such classic forms as bratwurst, frankfurters, and soft pretzels (if they're dry, we send 'em back). For dessert, there's Black Forest cake and

Hot Tip

La Cava de Tequila, inside Mexico's pyramid, is a cozy lounge featuring 95 varieties of tequila and a few mouth-watering appetizers. It's a great spot for a light meal. Reservations are not accepted here. Weekends are busiest.

apple strudel. The shaded outdoor seating area sports a festive mural. German wine and beer are offered at Sommerfest, located toward the rear of the Germany pavilion.

Tangierine Cafe (Morocco)

L D S | **$–$$** ♥

Named for the Moroccan city of Tangier, this casual spot serves (unremarkable) Mediterranean specialties—lentil salad, hummus, and tabbouleh, as well as rotisserie chicken and lamb presented as sandwiches (served on Moroccan bread) and combo platters (including a vegetarian option). Specialty coffees and pastries are available.

Hot Tip

The newest addition to the Italy pavilion is Tutto Gusto, a wine bar that transports guests to an ancient Italian wine cellar. Tutto Italia's neighbor offers more than 200 wines, including grappa; Italian beers and specialty drinks; coffee concoctions; and a small-plate menu. Reservations are not accepted—come in the afternoon for the smallest crowds. Salute!

Tutto Italia (Italy)

L D S | **$$–$$$** ♥

The menu has made Tutto Italia one of the most popular World Showcase restaurants, and the outdoor tables make it one of the more pleasant spots for dining at Epcot (when the weather cooperates, that is). Traditional starters such as fried calamari, fresh mozzarella with tomatoes and basil, and Caesar salad can make a meal in and of themselves. However, we recommend sampling the fresh pastas—made here daily—spaghetti, tagliatelle, lasagna, and more. Fish, pork, and chicken entrées round out the menu. At lunchtime, paninis are also an option—as is a selection of desserts.

🛎 Via Napoli (Italy)

L D S | **$$** | 🐭

Finally! A place to get pizza at Epcot's Italy. Located toward the back of the pavilion, this new 300-seat spot serves Neapolitan-style pizza, pastas, salads, sandwiches, soft drinks, and a selection of wines. How serious are they about pizza? They import the flour from Italy and select water so the crust tastes as authentically Neapolitan as possible. Reservations are recommended.

🍴 Yorkshire County Fish Shop (United Kingdom)

L D S | **$** | 🐭

A perfect choice for a snack or a light lunch, this stand offers scrumptious fish and chips. (Don't forget the malt vinegar.) Cola, iced tea, light lemonade, and Bass ale and Harp lager are also available. Shortbread cookies and bags of potato chips are sold here, too.

Hot Tip

If you plan to see IllumiNations, know that the show takes place nightly at 9 P.M. Try to time it so your evening meal winds up no later than 8:45 P.M.—and tell your server when you arrive.

Hot Tip

The Disney Dining Plan does not include gratuity. Please don't forget to tip your servers at table-service eateries. Figure on about 18–20 percent (for good service).

CHECK, PLEASE!

Paying for a meal at Disney World is a piece of cake—especially if you have a Disney resort ID (and back it up with a major credit card upon check-in). Resort IDs are accepted by most restaurants on WDW property. Notable exceptions: eateries at the Swan and Dolphin resorts, some Downtown Disney spots, Hotel Plaza Boulevard resorts, and some snack carts. Simply hand it to the waiter or cashier, sign the bill (don't forget to add a tip where appropriate), and the charge will appear on your hotel statement at check-out.

Of course, there are other ways to pay the piper. In addition to U.S. currency, which is welcome everywhere, traveler's checks and major credit cards are accepted in most non-cart locations. Foreign currency is a no-no. Disney currency (aka Disney Dollars) works like cash in all Disney-owned-and-operated venues. Disney Gift Cards are accepted at most WDW-owned-and-operated establishments. (If you plan to pay with a gift card, tell your server when you place your order.)

Disney's Hollywood Studios

Lights, camera, lunch! This theme park, designed to resemble a working Hollywood backlot circa the 1940s, tackles the role of feeding guests with style and whimsy. Here you can sit in a classic car and enjoy a meal at a drive-in, rub elbows with the beautiful people at a reproduction of the Hollywood Brown Derby, and play the part of sitcom kid as you're served by "Mom" or "Dad" at the 50's Prime Time Cafe (no elbows on the table, please!). While the attention to theming is obvious, it doesn't upstage the fare. So grab a napkin, and get ready for your close-up.

ABC Commissary

D S **$–$$** ♥

Located near the Chinese Theatre, this spot has shaken up the menu a few times of late. Most recently, it featured fish and chips, cheeseburgers, chicken curry, and an Asian salad. Dessert items include strawberry parfait and chocolate mousse. Soft drinks and beer are served. Note that breakfast is no longer offered here. The restaurant is huge and does indeed resemble an actual studio commissary. We could do without the ads for ABC shows, which play on a continuous loop from TVs scattered throughout the dining area. Enough already!

Backlot Express

D S **$–$$** ♥

Designed to look like a crafts shop on an old studio backlot, this eatery is near the Star Tours attraction. The indoor seating areas carry out the prop-shop theme, with paint-speckled floors, car engines, and various other spare prop parts. Outdoor tables are situated amid plants and trees. Menu offerings include burgers, chicken nuggets, hot dogs, grilled turkey and cheese sandwiches, grilled veggie sandwiches, and salads. For dessert, there's marble cheesecake and strawberry parfait. Soft drinks and beer are available.

50's Prime Time Cafe

L D **$$–$$$** ♥

This retreat to the era of *I Love Lucy* is an amusing amalgam of comfort food, kitschy 1950s-style kitchen nooks, and attentive servers of the "No talking with your mouth full" ilk. Nostalgia abounds, with more cookie

FANTASMIC! DINNER PACKAGE

Guests who make dining arrangements at their Disney resort or at any of the parks can take advantage of the Fantasmic! Dining Opportunity Special. Reserved seating for the evening's performance of Fantasmic! comes with the meal at no extra cost.

Why book the package? Besides guaranteeing a seat for dinner (lunch is offered seasonally), it ensures that you will get seating for Fantasmic! without having to wait in line. This is critical—since guests start lining up for the show as much as two hours ahead. With the package, you can have a relaxing dinner and head over to the show shortly before it starts.

Call 407-939-3463 for info or to book a "dinner and a show" package. At press time, the Hollywood Brown Derby, Hollywood & Vine, and Mama Melrose's Ristorante Italiano were participating in the program. (The Fantasmic! Dining Opportunity *may* be available for walk-ups, but we highly recommend booking it in advance—you've got nothin' to lose!)

jars than you could shake an Oreo at, all meant to bring you back to childhood of yesteryear; even the dessert menu is read on a View-Master, and TVs broadcast black-and-white clips from favorite fifties comedies (all related to food). Guests are waited on by "Mom" (and other family members) with considerable enthusiasm: They encourage everyone to keep their elbows off the table, eat their vegetables, and clean their plates (or no dessert!). Misbehave and you may have to stand in the corner (the 1950s "time out").

Adding to the appeal is the menu, which is packed with comfort foods. For openers, there's a choice of homemade chicken noodle soup or onion rings. Specialties of the house include magnificent meat loaf, served with mashed potatoes and vegetables; fried chicken; and old-fashioned pot roast. There are Caesar salads and chicken pot pie, too. Milk shakes, ice-cream sodas, and root beer floats are filling accompaniments. And when you've finished everything on your plate, you may order dessert. Stand-outs include s'mores—graham crackers topped with chocolate and toasted marshmallows—sundaes, seasonal cobbler, and no-sugar-added cheesecake topped with whipped cream and strawberry sauce. A full bar is available. Kids of all ages love this place. Reservations are recommended.

Hollywood & Vine
B L D **$$$**

The exterior is Art Deco, and the interior conjures up memories of a 1950s American diner—forged out of stainless steel with pink accents. It's next door to the 50's Prime Time Cafe, just off Hollywood Boulevard.

BABY NEEDS

Babies. They're a needy lot. Fortunately, most of the requisite supplies can be found somewhere at Disney World—if you know where to look. Formula and jarred food can be purchased at the Baby Care Center in each of the theme parks and at every WDW resort. Most restaurants have kids' menus with toddler-friendly food (mac and cheese, chicken nuggets, and the like).

If your baby is partial to a specific formula or brand of food, consider shipping a box of it to your hotel before you leave home. Keep in mind that there are several grocery stores near Disney World. If you'll have a car, it is worth the trip (a guest relations clerk can offer directions). The selections are more varied, as are the prices. Stash perishables in an in-room refrigerator—they rent for about $10 per night in WDW "value" resorts and are free in the "deluxe" and "moderate" resorts. It's best to request one when you make your reservation. Some other points of interest regarding baby diners at WDW:
• Most eateries have high chairs and booster seats. Request one when you make your restaurant reservation.
• Stroller use inside restaurants is discouraged. Park it outside.

Continued on page 58

DISNEY'S HOLLYWOOD STUDIOS

Continued from page 57

- WDW restaurants are often chilly. Be sure to pack a sweater or blanket.
- Be it a fast-food or table-service restaurant, bring toys to keep the little one(s) busy.
- The following resorts have 24-hour snack bars: Grand Floridian, Dolphin, Polynesian, Wyndham, and Buena Vista Palace (on Hotel Plaza Boulevard). The middle-of-the-night pickin's may be slim, but milk and cereal are served 'round the clock.
- If you'd like a quiet spot to nurse an infant, head to a Baby Care Center in any of the theme parks. They all have rooms with rocking chairs.
- If you're headed for a long day in a theme park, pack simple, healthy snacks for toddlers.
- To make your dining experience less harried, consider feeding your baby before you get to the restaurant.

The buffet breakfast and lunch, known as Disney Junior Play 'n Dine, are character affairs featuring June from *Little Einsteins*, Special Agent Oso, Jake the Never Land pirate, and Handy Manny. The morning meal includes Mickey waffles, frittatas, fruit, and pastries. Lunch may offer items such as salmon with maple mustard glaze, multigrain pasta with red-pepper pesto, and salads. Dinner, which is character-free, also features carved meats, peel-and-eat shrimp, and mussels. Some soft drinks are included. Reservations are recommended.

Hot Tip

If you can stand to miss the evening's performance of Fantasmic! (Disney's Hollywood Studios nighttime spectacular), consider dining in one of the park's popular eateries during the show.

☛ Hollywood Brown Derby
L D **$$–$$$** ❧

The Studios' most gracious dining is found at this faithful revival of the original *cause célèbre,* which opened on Hollywood and Vine in 1926. Dressed to the nines in chandeliers and celebrity caricatures, the restaurant stokes the appetite with its ever-so-finely chopped signature Cobb salad (invented by Brown Derby owner Bob Cobb) and grapefruit cake—a Brown Derby institution. Some of the fare is a bit highbrow (and high-priced) for the theme park crowd, but if you're up for a splurge, this spot is sure to rise to the occasion. We recommend the black grouper; the filet mignon gets good marks, too.

The slightly formal atmosphere is not likely to enchant most kids, but youngster-friendly fare is available. The New World wine list is excellent. Reservations are recommended.

☛ Mama Melrose's Ristorante Italiano
L D **$$–$$$** ❧

This pleasant Italian restaurant (with a California twist) is located in a large warehouse that has been converted into a dining room. Flatbreads are prepared in a wood-burning oven. The menu also features grilled fish, house-made pasta, and vegetarian options. Dishes include sautéed clams and pancetta tossed with spaghetti and white clam sauce, and oven-baked chicken parmigiana, plus soups and salads. The wine list includes selections from California and Italy. Reservations are recommended.

🍽 Min and Bill's Dockside Diner
S **$**

Mmm . . . milk shakes. 'Nuf said. In addition to some of the greatest, thickest chocolate and vanilla shakes in the World, Min and Bill's waterside snack spot also serves sausage sandwiches, hot dogs in pretzel rolls, chicken Caesar salads, cookies, soft drinks, and beer. To find it, look for the boat with the line to board, er, buy.

FYI: *Min and Bill* was a 1930s feature film (one of the first talkies) that took place on a waterfront. Hence, the lakefront locale.

🍽 Oasis Canteen
S **$**

A tiny tin shack that sits beside the Indiana Jones Epic Stunt Spectacular, the Oasis Canteen dispenses funnel cakes, waffle cones, bottled water, and draft beer.

🍽 Pizza Planet
L D S **$-$$** 🐭

Located inside a kid-magnet arcade, this is a counter-service spot with a limited but youngster-friendly menu. Select from simple individual pizzas (vegetarian, cheese, or pepperoni), meatball subs, salads, cookies, apple slices, cappuccino cupcakes, and soft drinks (including milk and apple juice). There is outdoor seating.

While the Sci-Fi Dine-In Theater has tables that can accommodate guests who use wheelchairs, there aren't many. Be sure to request such a table when you make your reservations—and confirm it by phone before you go; 407-WDW-DINE (939-3463).

Sci-Fi Dine-In Theater

L D **$$-$$$**

A convincing re-creation of a drive-in theater, the atmosphere here is completely absorbing. The tables are actually flashy, 1950s-era cars, complete with fins and whitewalls. Stars twinkle overhead in the "night sky," and drive-in theater speakers are mounted beside each car. Most seats are within cars, with most featuring front- and backseat counters facing front. Not terribly conducive to meaningful table talk, but ideal for viewing the large movie screen, where a 45-minute compilation of the best (and worst) of science-fiction trailers and cartoons plays in a continuous loop. There are a couple of traditional tables within oversize cars—if this is your preference, make that known when you book the table and expect to wait a bit when you arrive.

Selections include Reuben sandwiches, chicken sandwiches, burgers, and shrimp pasta. Kids enjoy the Mickey-plate pizza. Desserts include cheesecake, milk shakes, and ice-cream sundaes. It's popular with all ages, but some kids get spooked by the monsters in the movie clips. There are a few tables that accommodate guests using wheelchairs. Reservations are recommended.

 Starring Rolls Cafe
B L S **$–$$**

In a hurry? Here's where you can get the day off to a quick start, or take a coffee break. Pastries, bagels, muffins, croissants, and whole fruits are sold at this sweet-smelling shop. Coffee (beans are ground on-site), tea, and soft drinks are also served. For lunch, sandwiches, sushi, and wine are available. This spot usually closes at 4 P.M.

Studio Catering Co.
L D S **$–$$**

Next to the Honey, I Shrunk the Kids Movie Set Adventure, this spot offers sandwiches (vegetarian, buffalo chicken, turkey club, and more) and Greek salads. There is a full bar serving specialty libations, too.

Sunset Ranch Market
B L D S **$–$$**

A celebration of California's outdoor lifestyle, this open-air cluster of snack stands has something for everyone. **Rosie's All-American Cafe** sells cheeseburgers, veggie burgers, chicken breast nuggets, salads, and soups. **Catalina Eddie's** offers plain and pepperoni pizzas, hot Italian deli-style sandwiches, salads, chocolate-fudge cake, and carrot cake. Fruit, carrots, pretzels, granola bars, pickles, soft drinks, and frozen margaritas are available at **Anaheim Produce**. **Toluca Legs Turkey Co.** serves (enormous) turkey legs. **Hollywood Scoops Ice Cream** offers creamy treats (including one sugar-free flavor). **Fairfax Fare** features smoked specialties, including ribs and chicken, hot dogs, and breakfast selections (pastries and sandwiches).

Disney's Animal Kingdom

Walt Disney World's nature-oriented theme park is ideal for grazers: with more than a dozen spots to nosh, it may not be strong on table service (there are three such eateries), but it takes "quick service" quite seriously. When your stomach starts growling like the beasts at the Kilimanjaro Safaris attraction, consider the top-notch Tusker House and Flame Tree Barbecue. Not only do they offer mouth-watering meals, but they serve them in some of the fanciest theme park dining environments around.

Anandapur Ice Cream Truck

S **$**

This ice-cream truck doesn't actually move, but the Asia-based vehicle does deliver chilly treats. Ice cream is available by the cone or in a soda float.

Dino Bite Snacks

S **$** ♥

In DinoLand U.S.A., on the far side of Chester and Hester's DinoRama, is a small stand that offers ice cream (hand-dipped scoops, sundaes, floats, etc.), cookies (chocolate chip and oatmeal), chips, churros, and other snacks throughout the day.

Flame Tree Barbecue

L **D S** **$–$$** ♥

If you can't find this eatery, just follow your nose. Because when the kitchen is cooking, the scent is compelling. It serves up a selection of barbecued sandwiches and platters, all wood roasted. Sample the mild, tomato-based barbecue sauce or the spicy, mustard-based Carolina-style sauce with your chicken, pulled pork, or hickory-smoked St. Louis ribs. Disney's ovens produce 1,200 pounds at a time. (Would you like the recipe? Just ask!) Smoked turkey sandwiches, BBQ chicken salads, fruit plates (served with honey yogurt), fries, onion rings, and chocolate or Key lime mousse round out the options. Beer, wine, and soft drinks are served. There's outdoor seating along the river (which is quite lovely when it's not 98 degrees). If Flame Tree isn't serving, the tables are still open for use. It's located on Discovery Island, near DinoLand.

🏃 Harambe Fruit Market

`S` `$`

Sometimes, a crunchy apple is just what the doctor—or the hungry theme park guest—ordered. Apples, among other healthy snacks, are available at this fruit stand near the entrance to Kilimanjaro Safaris. Water and sports drinks are sold here, too.

🏃 Kusafiri Coffee Shop & Bakery

`B S` `$`

The bakery next to Tusker House provides a steady stream of fresh-from-the-oven treats such as croissants, muffins, and other snacks, plus cappuccino and espresso.

🏃 Pizzafari

`L D S` `$-$$` 🔱

This big, colorful dining area has no-nonsense fare that tends to please young palates. Salads and hot Italian-style sandwiches are also on the menu. Animal murals decorate the walls of this restaurant, located on Discovery Island, near the bridge to Camp Minnie-Mickey.

🛎 Rainforest Cafe

`B L D S` `$$-$$$`

Animal Kingdom's original table-service restaurant is located at its front entrance. The atmosphere blends well with the theme park it borders. Environmentally conscious cuisine includes items like Planet Earth Pasta and the Plant Sandwich. (The Big Blue Crab Delight—creamy dip loaded with crab meat and served with tortilla chips—is consistently yummy.) There's no net-caught fish on the menu, nor beef from countries that destroy rainforest land to raise cattle. Fish tanks, tropical decor, and the occasional thunderstorm add to the ambience (and noise level). Kids thrive here.

The restaurant and bar are accessible from inside and outside Animal Kingdom, so admission to the park isn't necessary to enter. Reservations are recommended for all meals.

WATER PARK DINING

Disney's duo of water parks, Typhoon Lagoon and Blizzard Beach, provides plenty of opportunities to defy Mom's plea to wait an hour to splash after you nosh. The fare is limited to the quick-service kind (who wants a sit-down meal in a soggy swimsuit?), and the quality of the offerings has been stepped up a bit of late. Typhoon Lagoon offers hot Italian sandwiches, fresh fruit bowls, meatball subs, and more. At Blizzard Beach, we're partial to the tomato-mozzarella sandwich and hot dogs wrapped in pretzel dough. Snacks are sold at spots with names like Typhoon Tilly's (**❤**), Leaning Palms (**❤**), and Avalunch (**❤**). Frozen drink specialties flow at Let's Go Slurpin' (Typhoon Lagoon) and at Blizzard Beach's Polar Bear Pool Bar.

Some folks prefer to pack a picnic lunch. Coolers may be brought into both parks, but alcoholic beverages and glass containers may not.

 Restaurantosaurus
L D S **$-$$** 🐭

Hang a right once you enter DinoLand U.S.A.
and you'll discover this spot. Themed as a
campsite for student paleontologists, this
eatery is filled with fossils, with class notes
lining the walls. The kitchen offers fast food
at lunch and dinner: hamburgers, veggie
subs, salad, and hot dogs—plus french fries,
chicken nuggets, and kids' meals.

Royal Anandapur Tea Co.
S **$**

After hiking through Africa to get to Asia,
guests can build up quite a thirst. That's
where this exotic tea stand comes in handy.
Located near the Yak & Yeti, this spot has a
variety of iced and hot teas, fruit smoothies,
specialty coffees, and sweet treats.

Tamu Tamu Refreshments
S **$**

This window dispenses cheeseburgers, turkey
sandwiches, tandoori chicken salad, and
shakes. There's a seating nook next door. It's
in Harambe, across from Tusker House.

Tusker House
B L D S **$-$$** 🐭

The Tusker House fare—which is offered
buffet style—is head, shoulders, and antlers
above the rest. It's on the left side of
Harambe, just over the bridge from Discovery
Island. Donald Duck fans are especially
pleased with the addition of Donald's Safari
Breakfast buffet. It's offered daily and
includes visits from the aforementioned

fowl, plus Mickey, Daisy, and Goofy. Breakfast runs from 8 A.M. until 10:30 A.M., while lunch and dinner are offered from 11:30 A.M. till the park's posted closing time. Reservations are recommended. The Kusafiri Coffee Shop & Bakery operates from a window outside.

Trilo-Bites
S **$**

This little cabin, located just inside the entrance to DinoLand, sells smoked turkey legs, frozen lemonade, and soft drinks.

Yak & Yeti
L D S **$$–$$$** 🎦

Grab a set of chopsticks and dig in! This elaborate venue is a much-welcome addition to the small Animal Kingdom family of table-service eateries. Nestled deep in the park's village of Anandapur (across from the entrance to the Kali River Rapids attraction), the restaurant—which opens at 10 A.M.—specializes in Asian-fusion cuisine. Reservations are recommended. Its shop offers goods ranging from sushi plates to fine teapots. There is a quick-service area nearby. It serves lunch and dinner.

Hot Tip

Do you have a WDW Annual Pass? If so, know that many Disney World eateries offer lunchtime discounts for you and up to three guests. Lunch hours vary from place to place, and alcohol is not included. Inquire when you make your reservations.

Downtown Disney

This enclave of shopping, dining, and entertainment has three distinct neighborhoods: the Marketplace, Pleasure Island, and the West Side. Within them, you'll find eateries such as Wolfgang Puck Café, House of Blues, Ghirardelli Ice Cream & Chocolate Shop, Planet Hollywood, Rainforest Cafe, and T-Rex: A Prehistoric Family Adventure. Overall, Downtown Disney provides a variety of fast food, table service, cheap eats, and super splurges. Downtown Disney is on Walt Disney World property and can be reached by car, resort bus, or ferry (from select WDW resorts). Note that all branches of Downtown Disney's entertaining triumvirate are gate- and admission-free.

Hot Tip

DisneyQuest devotees note: The venue's resident Cheesecake Factory Express is no more. However, you can still tame that appetite you built up after hours of gaming without leaving the confines of DisneyQuest. An eatery called FoodQuest has taken over the space formerly occupied by C.F.E. Admission must be paid to enter DisneyQuest before you can eat at the quick-service restaurant. It serves lunch, dinner, and snacks—and participates in the Disney Dining Plan.

Bongos Cuban Cafe (West Side)

L D S $$-$$$

Spicing up the Downtown Disney dining repertoire with a menu driven by Cuban and Latin American flavors, this eatery was created, in part, by singer Gloria Estefan. Its slate of traditional and nouvelle Cuban dishes includes black bean soup (our preferred dish), plantains, steak topped with onions, and flan. The atmosphere here is quite lovely (and often lively). Indoors, the mosaic mural and palm-leaf railings set the scene; the patio for outdoor seating wraps around a three-story pineapple, easily our favorite part of this creatively designed restaurant. A take-out window provides snacks on the go. Diners are sometimes treated to live music (feel free to sway in your seat). A small shop sells items such as shirts and hats emblazoned with the Bongos logo. Reservations are available by calling 407-828-0999.

Cap'n Jack's Restaurant (Marketplace)

L D S **$$-$$$** ❤

The Cap'n is a true Disney World legend, having the distinction of 30-plus years of seafaring service under his cap. His fare, like his look, remains timeless. The nautically themed pier house juts right out over Village Lake, providing water views from most vantage points. The appetizer menu is such—shrimp, clam chowder, and the like—that it's as good for lunch or dinner as it is for a snack. Entrées extend to jumbo lump crab cakes, salmon, pot roast, pasta dishes, and seafood specialties. There is a tempting variety of wines, beer, and other cocktails—and the house's signature frozen strawberry margaritas are classic.

Cap'n Jack's is a nice place to enjoy the late afternoon, as the setting sun streams through the picture windows. Reservations are recommended.

Earl of Sandwich (Marketplace)

B L D S **$-$$** ❤

This tip-top counter-service establishment is brimming with sweet and savory possibilities. Among the fare standing by is a variety of hot and cold sandwiches (freshly prepared on warm bread), wraps, tossed salads, and homemade desserts. More exotic selections, such as Hawaiian BBQ (Hawaiian BBQ ham with fresh pineapple and Swiss cheese), The Original 1762 (warm roast beef sandwich with creamy horseradish sauce and cheddar cheese), and Caribbean Jerk Chicken are served, too. The Veggie sandwich is also an option.

Breakfast items include sandwiches and baked goods. There are quite a few "grab and go" selections as well. Dessert can be cupcakes, fresh-baked cookies, muffin crowns, or English trifle. Beer, wine, and Kona coffee are on the menu, too. Ample seating is available inside the Earl of Sandwich eatery and at outdoor tables.

Fulton's Crab House (Pleasure Island)

L D S $$$–$$$$

This regal restaurant, originally known as the *Empress Lilly* (after Walt Disney's wife, Lillian Disney), occupies a three-deck riverboat. Though it looks as if it might set sail at any moment, the replica ship is permanently docked at the edge of Village Lake (near Portobello). Guests board the ship via gangway and are enveloped by polished woods, brass detailing, and nautical nostalgia.

The extensive (albeit pricey) dinner menu changes with the day's arrivals. It's not unusual for Alaskan wild halibut to be seen next to Panama City (Florida) snapper. Signature seafood dishes include Dungeness crab legs; a San Francisco-style seafood stew with king crab, shrimp, scallops, mussels, and fish in a tomato broth; and crab and lobster platters. For landlubbers, bone-in rib-eye, filet mignon, and free-range chicken are satisfying choices.

For a quicker fix, visit our top choice here: the ravishing raw bar at the adjoining Stone Crab lounge. In fact, for a relatively reasonably priced lunch, it's lounge or bust. If the weather's pleasant, try for a table outside, on the bow of the ship. Reservations are recommended for the restaurant.

🏃 Ghirardelli Ice Cream & Chocolate Shop (Marketplace)

S **$-$$**

What is it about an old-fashioned ice cream parlor that makes just about everybody giddy? Oh, yes, the ice cream. This spot does it one better and throws in its famous chocolate, to boot. Stop in for a chocolatey treat, root beer float, or a malt. Tables are available on a first-come, first-served basis. There is a walk-up counter, too. We often duck in here for a quick cup of coffee and a chocolate chaser. And there's always the potential for a free candy sample.

🍴 House of Blues (West Side)

D S **$$-$$$**

Thanks to the combination of its diverse menu and rustic, folk art-studded design, this Disney-based House of Blues doesn't disappoint. Favorites include flatbreads (grilled then finished in the pizza oven), lobster mac and cheese, tacos, corn bread, and jambalaya. At the far west of the West Side, H.O.B. is a good choice for a satisfying meal or a late-night bite. Live music is presented in the restaurant and on the front porch on select days. There is a lively gospel brunch every Sunday. Reservations are recommended. To book a table at the House of Blues, call 407-934-BLUE (934-2583).

🍴 Paradiso 37 (Pleasure Island)

D **$$-$$$** 🔴

This dynamic waterfront eatery specializes in "mangled margaritas," stocks 37 kinds of tequila, and boasts the "coldest beer in the world." Oh, and they serve food, too!

Paradiso 37's menu focuses on "street foods" of the Americas. Appetizer selections include the signature fire-roasted corn on the cob with a mild pepper sauce and cheese, mac and cheese bites, and potato pancakes. Entrées range from Argentinian skirt steak with chimichurri sauce to Chilean-style salmon and prickly pear shrimp salad. No reservations necessary.

🍽 Planet Hollywood (West Side)

▮ D S **$$–$$$** ✿

Chances are, you'll have no trouble finding this restaurant—just keep your eyes peeled for the giant globe. Built on three levels, this colossal sphere is jam-packed with classic movie and television memorabilia.

The menu features salads, sandwiches, pasta dishes, burgers, appetizers, fajitas, and dessert specialties. Consider sampling the chicken crunch appetizer, Asian chicken salad, shrimp and bacon club sandwich, or lasagna. Bananas Foster is among the dessert choices. Reservations are recommended.

🍽 Portobello (Pleasure Island)

▮ D **$$$**

This Italian trattoria is drenched in warm colors that match the rustic Italian cuisine. The best seats are on the waterfront porch, and the wood-burning-oven pizzas are still a top choice. Traditional Italian cuisine includes mix-and-match antipasti, hand-crafted sausage, pastas, and fish.

At lunchtime, the menu includes Portobello's signature sandwiches, like the pesto-marinated chicken with fontina cheese. For dinner, try the ravioli gigante (filled with ricotta and spinach) with tomato, basil, and toasted garlic. The full-service bar offers a solid wine list of Italian favorites, specialty cocktails, and beer. For dessert, it's tough to resist the tiramisu.

Raglan Road Irish Pub (Pleasure Island)

L D S $$–$$$

A wee bit of the Emerald Isle can be found at Disney's Pleasure Island. The convivial spot features furnishings crafted in Ireland, live music, and a menu with cuisine courtesy of Chef Kevin Dundon, one of Ireland's best-known culinary wizards. Think traditional Irish fare with a modern flair. Instead of plain old fish with your chips, expect lightly sautéed lemon sole. There is no charge to enter—be it for food or drink.

Rainforest Cafe (Marketplace)

L D S $$–$$$

Lush (and loud) as a jungle, this place is thick with tropical vegetation and fish-filled aquariums (not to mention the occasional thunderstorm). A talking tree offers a stream of ecological insights, and animal experts are on hand to field questions. Dishes have names like Mogambo (pasta with shrimp), Plant Sandwich (veggies), and Mojo Bones (barbecued ribs). Appetizers and desserts can be shared. Reservations can be made by calling the restaurant: 407-827-8500. Without them, expect quite a wait. Note that there is another Rainforest Cafe at Disney's Animal Kingdom. The Animal Kingdom location accepts reservations through 407-WDW-DINE (939-3463).

🍴 T-Rex: A Prehistoric Family Adventure (Marketplace)

L D **$$–$$$**

Dinosaurs throw one heck of a dinner party. See for yourself at this eye-popping dino-themed, interactive feasting facility. When you enter, you'll be greeted by hosts we were all led to believe were extinct. Okay, they're life-size *mechanical* dinosaurs, but they're still pretty cool. As are the waterfalls, bubbling geysers, and fossil dig site. It's all so distracting, you may forget why you came here in the first place. When your stomach starts growling, plan to appease it with anything from Jurassic Salad to Prehistoric Pot Pie. With soup, sandwiches, pasta, seafood, and steaks, this place aims to please everyone. You'll find it near Fulton's Crab House at Downtown Disney Marketplace.

🏃 Wetzel's Pretzels (Marketplace and West Side)

S **$**

Salted or unsalted, buttery or plain—Wetzel's can satisfy most pretzel cravings. Among the choices are the Jalapeño Cheese Melt, the Sinful Cinnamon, and the Three-Cheese varieties. They sell ice cream, too.

🍴 Wolfgang Puck Café (West Side)

L D S **$$$** 🐭

One of four Walt Disney World establishments that bear the name Wolfgang Puck, this one offers some of the chef's best-known specialties. Among the spotlighted dishes are pizzas, Thai chicken satay, pasta with fresh vegetables, Chinois chicken salad, and rotisserie chicken. The menu is equal parts sophisticated and straightforward—and very fresh. Plan ahead and save room for dessert. The place is a bit noisy and showing signs of age, but still has its fans.

Sushi lovers take note: Housed within this space is a sushi bar that's as aesthetically appealing as it is palate-pleasing. You can order sushi at the bar and in the cafe. Reservations are recommended for the cafe.

☝🍽 Wolfgang Puck Café— The Dining Room (West Side)
D $$$-$$$$

Don't be confused by the name. The Dining Room refers to a separate restaurant that just happens to be in the same building as Wolfgang Puck Café and Express. (We think of it as "Puck's Deluxe.") The formal upstairs Dining Room is devoted to more of Wolfgang Puck's cuisine—for example, Chinois rack of lamb with a spicy cilantro-mint sauce and garlic mashed potatoes. Reservations are recommended.

🏃 Wolfgang Puck Express (Marketplace and West Side)
L D S $-$$ 🐭

Wolfgang Puck turns his talents to fast service and signature treats. Among them are (delectable) wood-fired pizzas, rotisserie chicken, soups, sandwiches, grown-up-friendly mac and cheese, and salads—including his famous Chinois chicken salad. (The West Side location is tucked inside the Wolfgang Puck Café building, while the Marketplace spot is near the Disney's Days of Christmas shop.)

ATTENTiON, COFFEE SNOBS

Face it. For many of us, the magic doesn't start until that first sip of coffee makes its way past our lips. And not just any coffee will do. It must be a half-caf latte with extra foam! In other words, we have great expectations. The bad news? The standard cup here is Nescafé. If you're a fan, you're in luck. If not, you'll have to venture a bit to get a satisfying java jolt. The good news is, specialty coffee bars—including Starbucks—are easing their way onto the Disney scene. There's at least one in each theme park and some at the resorts. Select restaurants serve special coffee blends, too. Among our favorite spots:

- American Adventure (Epcot's World Showcase, a stand near the pavilion)
- Artist Point (Wilderness Lodge)
- Big River Grille & Brewing Works (BoardWalk resort)
- California Grill (Contemporary resort)
- Contemporary resort (lobby stand)
- Flying Fish Cafe (BoardWalk resort)
- 40 Thirst Street (Downtown Disney Marketplace and West Side)
- Fresh—Mediterranean Market (Dolphin resort)
- Garden Grove (Swan resort)
- Jiko—The Cooking Place (Animal Kingdom Lodge)
- Kona Cafe (Polynesian resort)
- Kouzzina by Cat Cora (BoardWalk resort)
- Picabu (Dolphin resort)

WDW RESORTS

Each of the nearly 30 resorts at Walt Disney World offers its own set of specially themed eateries. There are clambakes at the Beach Club, luaus at the Polynesian, wild game at the Wilderness Lodge, and beignets at Port Orleans French Quarter. Meals may be served buffet, family, or traditional table-service or fast-food style. Disney characters are often on hand (especially for breakfast), and some snack spots stay open 'round the clock. In fact, the resort dining scene has expanded and been upgraded so much of late that the (occasionally arduous) task of resort-hopping is a more worthwhile experience than ever before.

ALL-STAR RESORTS

🏃 Food Courts
B L D S $–$$ 🎃

Each of the All-Star resorts features a themed central food court. **All-Star Sports** has **End-Zone** food court in **Stadium Hall**. At **All-Star Music**, it's **Intermission** food court in **Melody Hall**. And at the **All-Star Movies** resort, it is the **World Premiere** food court in **Cinema Hall**. The food courts offer similar food stands—although Movies is a cut above. (It's a bit bigger, brighter, and more modern.) The selections include pasta, pizza, burgers, hot dogs, sandwiches, salads, snacks, and a wide variety of break- fast and baked goods, plus a selection of "grab and go" items. Expect to find lots of kid-pleasers.

ANIMAL KINGDOM LODGE

🍽 Boma—Flavors of Africa
B D $$–$$$ 🎃

Designed to resemble an African market- place, Boma offers an impressively diverse selection—the fare served represents the 53 countries that make up Africa. Though the eatery may be described as "cafeteria style," this is not a negative. It's one big buffet with multiple stations, and the food is as good as what you'd expect in a fine dining place.

The all-you-can-eat affair provides an excellent bang for your Disney dining buck. Menu selections include wood-roasted meats

B *breakfast*   **L** *lunch*   **D** *dinner*   **S** *snacks*

WDW RESORTS

and seafood, plus African-inspired soups, a decidedly different watermelon rind salad, and vegetarian offerings. Be sure to leave room for the decadent pastry known as the Amarula Zebra Dome. It's tempting to overeat at a bounteous feast such as this, so consider taking tiny portions of everything. You can go back for seconds of your favorites. The wine list includes selections from various African vineyards. Even if you're not staying at the Lodge, it's worth the trip. Reservations are recommended.

Jiko—The Cooking Place

D $$$–$$$$ ❤

Here at one of the most unusual Walt Disney World dining experiences, Jiko's cuisine is inspired by the tastes of Africa, with influences from around the globe. Start with one of the paper-thin flatbreads (like African-spiced fire-roasted chicken with four cheeses and bacon), grilled wild boar tenderloin, artisan cheeses, or seasonal salads. Kenyan coffee-rubbed fish is a signature dish, and you may find grilled shrimp curry; braised beef short ribs; seared duck breast; and oak-grilled filet mignon on the menu, too. End your meal with a fabulous cheese course, and/or sweets such as coconut bread pudding or a Tanzanian chocolate and Kenyan coffee mousse.

The impressive wine list is exclusively South African, one of the most extensive collections in the U.S. This is an excellent choice for a grown-up splurge. Though it's hardly a kid favorite (the international, sometimes exotic cuisine may not appeal to timid palates), there are child-friendly options on the kids' menu. Reservations are recommended. Incidentally, the word *jiko* is Swahili for "the cooking place."

The Mara

B L D S $-$$ 🐭

This place has a couple of stations at which hot entrée selections are prepared. There's a "grab and go" department, too. Among the pre-packaged options are sandwiches, salads, fruit, and baked goods.

Sanaa

L D $$-$$$ 🐭

Pronounced *sah-NAH*, the name of this eatery means "artwork" in Swahili. The Kidani Village spot has a family-friendly menu featuring Disney's take on African-Indian cuisine. Signature dishes include chicken or shrimp curry and beef short ribs slow-cooked in tandoor ovens. For lunch, try the salad sampler. Even the burgers have an Indian touch, wrapped in soft, warm *naan* (a round flatbread). The breads with chutneys, pickles, and raita (yogurt dip) are superb. Desserts introduce many tastes, from no-sugar-added mango pudding to cardamom butter cake. Reservations are recommended.

ART OF ANIMATION

🏃 LANDSCAPE OF FLAVORS

B L D S $-$$ 🐭

"Better-for-you" options is the theme of this vividly adorned food court, where everything is made fresh as it is ordered. Four mini shops offer soups, salads, pizza, sandwiches, fresh fruit smoothies, organic teas, beer (including gluten-free), wine, coffee, and juices. Pizzas may be delivered to guestrooms in the resort.

BOARDWALK

🍽 Big River Grille & Brewing Works
L D S | **$$–$$$** | 🍴

A standout for its fresh-brewed ales alone, this unassuming place delivers huge portions of pub grub. The straightforward-but-satisfying menu generally includes burgers and steaks. Sandwiches are a cut above. This restaurant tends to be more low-key than other BoardWalk eateries and makes for a peaceful retreat during the day. The interior has a nice, pubby feel. We like to sit at outdoor tables on the boardwalk. Seating is available on a first-come, first-served basis.

🏃 BoardWalk Bakery
B L D S | **$** | 🍴

On any given morning, there are lines out the door of this tiny bakeshop next door to Kouzzina by Cat Cora. (If you're staying at the BoardWalk resort, this is one of the places to get your morning Nescafé.) The menu of fresh-baked goods includes muffins, croissants, and cookies. They have sandwiches and salads, too.

🍽 ESPN Club
L D S | **$$–$$$** | 🍴

For sports fans, this joint is nothing short of a miracle. The spacious, welcoming, occasionally frenzied bar/family restaurant is a hard-core sports club. If there's a game being played, chances are it's on one of the million (okay, hundred—but it feels like a lot more) TVs. If not, a simple request may result in a channel change.

The fare includes burgers, wings, grilled fish, sandwiches, and a variety of salads and other entrées. Both the dining room and the bar area serve the full menu. Note that this establishment does not accept reservations. If you want to get a good seat, get there long before game time.

🍽️ Flying Fish Cafe
D **$$$–$$$$** 🐭

Fun, sophisticated decor from the designer of the Contemporary's California Grill elevates the appeal—in fact, this restaurant could give most fine, big-city dining spots a run for their money. (Expect the tab to rival cosmopolitan hot spots, too.)

Chef Tim Keating is a wonderfully inventive chef, and his menu changes often. But you'll always find the signature potato-wrapped snapper with a creamy leek fondue and red wine and butter sauce, the crisp crab cakes, and a char-crusted New York strip steak. We are routinely impressed by the service and find the menu worthy of the price tag. Reservations are recommended. Diners *sans* reservations may ask to sit at the counter (when doing so, we prefer to sit by the open flames of the grill [shielded by safety glass, of course]—we enjoy the show).

🍽️ Kouzzina by Cat Cora
B D **$$–$$$** 🐭

The newest eatery on the BoardWalk block comes courtesy of celebrity chef Cat Cora (of *Iron Chef* fame). Mediterranean-style cuisine is the name of the game here. Breakfast includes Kouzzina's signature blend of press-pot coffee, and a delectable icy Greek frappé. In addition to Greek-style yogurt with fresh fruit and house-made granola, morning offerings include turkey-sweet potato hash with eggs and arugula salad; and spinach-tomato-feta scrambled eggs. Dinner starters include crisp calamari, goat-cheese-stuffed grape leaves, spinach pie, and Greek salad. The main course menu offers cinnamon stewed chicken, wood-grilled rib-eye steak, and traditional whole fish. Consider such accompaniments as garlic-rosemary potatoes, sautéed brussel sprouts with capers and lemon, and herbed orzo with olive oil and cheese. Kids' selections include grilled fish and grilled chicken strips. Traditional baklava and dense, rich chocolate *budino* (pudding) are dessert favorites. Reservations are recommended.

Seashore Sweets'

S **$**

A cheery, old-fashioned sweetshop, this spot sells heavenly homemade candies, saltwater taffy, homemade ice cream, sorbet, and frozen yogurt. It's next door to the Flying Fish Cafe.

CARIBBEAN BEACH

Old Port Royale Food Court

B L D S **$–$$** 🐭

A cluster of side-by-side, walk-up windows, this basic food court caters to families. **Market Street Grab 'N Go** serves croissants, rolls, pastries, and other fresh-baked treats. Soups, salads, and hot and cold sandwiches make up the selections at **Montego's Deli**. Burgers and chicken sandwiches are among the many offerings at **Port Royale**

Hamburger Shop. In addition to pizza, the **Royale Pizza & Pasta Shop** serves Italian specialties. **Bridgetown Broiler Shop** serves made-to-order omelets for breakfast and a selection of dinner items, such as carved turkey and pork loin.

📌 Shutters at Old Port Royale

D S | **$$–$$$** | 🐭

The dining room here is as kid-friendly as a table-service eatery can be. Some menu highlights include New York strip steak, Caribbean pasta, and pork ribs. The restaurant is in the resort's Old Port Royale building, across from the food court. In addition to soft drinks, beer, wine, and cocktails are served. Reservations are recommended.

CONTEMPORARY

📌 California Grill

D | **$$$–$$$$** | 🐭

The West Coast theme shines through in such dishes as grilled pork tenderloin with goat cheese polenta, roasted mushrooms, Zinfandel glaze, and sage. The wine list is a mix of greatest hits and good finds. (At press time, several vintages were available by the glass.) Also drawing a crowd: the Grill's flatbreads, sushi bar, and a host of vegetarian choices. The goat-cheese ravioli appetizer is a favorite.

Fresh desserts along the lines of warm Valrhona chocolate cake provide the finishing touches, and there are sweeping views of the Magic Kingdom (from select seats).

The spectacular sushi bar, set within the restaurant, is always crowded and never fails to elicit raves. The din in the dining room may impede quiet conversation. Servers occasionally seem to be spread too thin, but the food is first-rate. Reservations are necessary and must be booked with a credit card. Changes or cancellations must be made at least 24 hours ahead to avoid the $20 per person fee. This is a Disney Dining Plan "signature" restaurant.

An outdoor perch (exclusively available to California Grill patrons) affords bird's-eye views of the Magic Kingdom. Guests (including those planning to visit the lounge or sushi bar) check in on the hotel's second floor and are escorted to the restaurant's express elevator. *At press time, California Grill was slated for a massive refurbishment and may not be open during your visit.*

Chef Mickey's

 **B D** **$$–$$$**

Sprawling across the cavernous fourth floor of the Contemporary is one of the biggest kid pleasers at Walt Disney World. Here, Chef Mickey and his friends host a very

---

IN-ROOM REFRIGERATORS

Hotel rooms in "deluxe" and "moderate" WDW resorts come with mini fridges. Guests staying at "value" resorts may rent a fridge for about $10 a night. Request it when you book the room, and confirm before arrival. They take up room, but the fridges are handy for milk and baby products, snacks, and small amounts of groceries. Guests who must refrigerate medical supplies will not be charged for refrigerator use (a copy of the prescription may be required).

popular buffet feast. The changing menu takes advantage of seasonal offerings; a sundae bar provides a sweet finish.

At some point during the meal, Chef Mickey will stop by your table, as will several of his friends. Be prepared to drop your fork and swing your napkin with Mickey on a moment's notice. Kids adore this place. Reservations are a must.

🏃 Contempo Café
B L D S $-$$ 🐭

If you head to the first floor in search of the snack bar that's been there since 1971, you're in for a surprise: It moved! All the way to the fourth floor. Peruse the menu on electronic boards with color photos, place your order, then head to the cashier. A pager blinks when food is ready for pick-up. (It's confusing for first-timers. Don't be shy about asking for guidance.) Thin-crust pizzas, sandwiches, and soups are among the selections. A "grab and go" section has drinks, salads, and fresh fruit.

🍽 The Wave . . . of American Flavors
B L D $$-$$$ 🐭

Casual and fun, The Wave brings a surge of dining ideas to Disney. Starting with organic Colombian coffee served with the bountiful buffet breakfast, you know this is going to be different. At lunch, seasonal soups, oversized salads, and a vegetarian sandwich vie for attention with a classic Reuben and a bison burger. At dinner, we highly recommend a lump crab cake starter, followed with the sustainable fish of the day or the locally sourced all-natural pork tenderloin. You can end on a sweet note with tempting desserts that include no-sugar-added options.

The wine program, with only screw-cap wines, focuses on bright-style New World wines (an impressive 50 choices are available by the glass). Beer fans get several craft beer selections available in flight samplers. Reservations are recommended. The cool adjacent lounge is perfect for an aperitif or after-dinner drink.

CORONADO SPRINGS

🍽️ Maya Grill

D **$$$** 🐭

Guests here dine inside a Mayan pyramid, beside a volcano (dormant, of course). The menu has a bit of everything: seafood, meat, and poultry, with a touch of Latino spices added to some of the creations. The pulled-pork empanada and pan-seared scallops with chorizo are interesting starts to dinner. Entrées range from rib-eye steak and pork chops Milanesa to grilled salmon, with many dishes cooked over an open-pit wood-fire grill. Dinner is usually served from 6 P.M. until 9 P.M. Reservations are recommended.

🏃 Pepper Market

B L D S **$-$$** 🐭

Modeled after an open-air market, this spot has a large seating area and many food stands to choose from. The concept here has been tweaked a bit—instead of wandering the food court-style stations and paying for individual selections, each meal is a set price and guests dine as if they were at a buffet. The "all you care to eat" selections

DINNER AT SEA

For Disney's ultimate dinner-and-a-show splurge, consider reserving the elegant *Grand I* yacht. You and up to 17 lucky invitees can enjoy a private tour of the lakes near the Magic Kingdom capped off with a viewing of Wishes, the park's fireworks show—all the while devouring delightful delicacies prepared by chefs at the Grand Floridian resort. The possibilities range from an intimate cruise for two, complete with dinner and champagne, to a swinging cocktail party for 18, with a boatload of shrimp, chips, wings, beer, and wine.

It costs about $520 (plus tax) per hour to rent the 5-room floating fantasyland. Driver and deckhand are included; refreshments are not. To book, call 407-WDW-PLAY at least 24 hours and up to 90 days ahead. The *Grand I* docks at the Grand Floridian but can pick up passengers at the Contemporary, Polynesian, and Wilderness Lodge.

range from roast beef (or pork or turkey) to paninis, pizza, pasta, salads, and Mexican fare—all prepared from scratch. Non-alcoholic drinks are included and anything can be ordered "to go." Everything is paid for at meal's end, as guests file past the cashier at the exit. Note that a ten percent gratuity is automatically included when you eat in the dining area. Given this resort's popularity with the convention set, expect a proliferation of people during weekday breakfast and lunch times. Specifics may change in 2013.

DISNEY'S OLD KEY WEST

🏃 Good's Food to Go

BLDS **$** ♥

A walk-up window with a simple menu: hamburgers, cheeseburgers, grilled chicken sandwiches, salads, ice cream, and breakfast selections are among the offerings.

🍽 Olivia's Cafe

BID **$–$$** ♥

We thoroughly enjoy the Key West manner with which Olivia's approaches its theme. The laid-back setting and menu convey the spirit of the leisure-centric locale. Breakfast includes standards, but also some interesting combos like shrimp and conch eggs Benedict. Later in the day, look for items such as salads, conch chowder, crab cakes, conch fritters, specialty sandwiches, and Key lime tart or banana bread pudding. Dinner can bring slow-roasted prime rib, fish, and pork chops to the table. Wine, beer, and cocktails are served. The menu changes seasonally. Reservations are recommended.

FORT WILDERNESS

🍽 Trail's End Restaurant

BLDS **$–$$** ♥

True, it's a bit out of the way for anyone but Fort Wilderness guests (and even for some of them!), but for many, this rustic and unassuming spot is well worth the trip.

The informal log-walled restaurant offers a hearty buffet breakfast. The fare is not exactly gourmet, but it is bountiful. Breakfast selections include grits, biscuits, gravy, and a tasty "breakfast pizza." The à la carte lunch offers fried chicken, waffles, sautéed catfish, and fried green tomatoes. For dinner, expect a buffet of smoked pork ribs, peel-and-eat shrimp, fried chicken, carved meats, a salad bar, and a variety of sides and dessert items. Pizza and light items are available nightly from 4 P.M. until 10 P.M. Beer, wine, and soft drinks are served. Reservations are recommended. Breakfast costs about $16 for adults, $10 for kids; lunch is à la carte; dinner is about $23 for adults, $13 for kids. After the meal, guests may chat and relax in rocking chairs on the porch. It's a bit off the WDW beaten path, but for many it's worth the trek—this place is quite the bargain.

GRAND FLORIDIAN

 **Cítricos**

D $$$–$$$$ 🐭

From the aromas wafting from the open kitchen, it's clear that the chef has vowed to wow you with cuisine from the Americas and the Mediterranean herb by fragrant herb. The fare varies seasonally, but may include such items as sautéed shrimp with tomato, lemon, and feta cheese; or braised veal shank. Adventurous palates are most at home here. The menu's not extensive, but the wine list is. There is a private party room for parties of up to 12. Food may be ordered in the lounge, too (ask the bartender for a menu). Reservations are recommended.

ONE LUMP OR TWO?

Teatime with all the à la carte trim-
mings—scones, tiny sandwiches, and
pastries served on bone china— is at
2 P.M. in the Garden View Tea Room at
the Grand Floridian. A large selection
of teas (some custom blends are made
exclusively for this establishment) and
tasty accompaniments are offered
every day until approximately 4:30 P.M.
Reservations are recommended.

Gasparilla Grill & Games
B L D S $-$$

The mainstays at this 24-hour snack bar near
the marina are grilled chicken, burgers,
pizza, hot dogs, and soft serve ice cream.
Fruit, cereal, packaged snacks, soft drinks,
beer, and wine are also available. We prefer
to eat outdoors beside the marina, as
opposed to noshing next to the noisy arcade
games. Items may be ordered "to go."
Continental breakfast is also available.

Grand Floridian Cafe
B L D $$$

A pleasant spot any time of day (there's so
much old-world atmosphere here, you'd
almost expect to see ladies twirling parasols
in the midday sun and Scott Joplin playing
"The Entertainer" on a grand piano), the
cafe is a relatively reasonably priced, low-key
way to check out the poshest WDW resort.

The à la carte breakfast extends a bit
beyond the usual fare. Lunch and dinner menus
vary with the season but have traditional

American dishes: onion soup, burgers, and the signature Grand Floridian sandwich. The wine selection is excellent. Reservations are recommended, but it may be possible to get a table if you're willing to wait. The restaurant is closed between 11 A.M. and 11:45 A.M.

Narcoossee's
D **$$$–$$$$**

Named for a nearby Central Florida town, Narcoossee's specializes in fresh fish dishes —with the occasional land-based entrée making surf-and-turf combinations a decadent possibility. Narcoossee's menu has upscale selections (and prices), but the atmosphere is casual and, more than occasionally, clamorous. The display kitchen presents dishes such as steamed mussels, wild salmon, and Maine lobster. The international wine selection is quite good— you might even enjoy a pre-dinner glass on the veranda. The view of the Seven Seas Lagoon and the Magic Kingdom (in the distance) completes the experience. Reservations are recommended.

1900 Park Fare
B D **$$$**

The atmosphere is reminiscent of an old-time amusement park, but the sophisticated buffet menu and subtle decor make this one of the most elegant character restaurants on the property. Mary Poppins and friends (characters vary) mingle with guests during the bountiful daily breakfast. Cinderella and her cronies visit the dining room during the dinner hours. Keep in mind that the lineup of characters does change from time to time.

Dinner features hot and cold seafood,

pastas, vegetables, breads, and prime rib. The offerings change weekly, and some may be customized. A salad bar and dessert bar stand nearby. There's a special kids' buffet, too. It offers pizza, pasta, and assorted vegetables. The restaurant's focal point is Big Bertha, a band organ built in Paris nearly a century ago. She sits in a proscenium and rises 15 feet above the floor, occasionally bursting into a musical serenade. Reservations are recommended.

Victoria & Albert's

D $$$$

This elegant dining room has the distinction of being Central Florida's only five-diamond restaurant, an honor awarded by AAA. It is indulgent without being too haute to handle (although the steep prices may curb your enthusiasm) and is considered by many to be the *grande dame* of the Disney dining scene.

The seven-course prix fixe menu changes often, always offering a selection of fish, poultry, and beef as main courses. But the beauty of this high-end experience is all the little tastes as you make your way through the $125-per-person adventure. You might start with lobster or quail, then move on to seared wild turbot or pork tenderloin. The cheese course is worth every calorie. And, even with seven courses, you must reserve room for the indulgent desserts: a flurry of soufflés, chocolate, and more. Perfect portions keep it all surprisingly manageable. The strains of a harp or violin provide a romantic backdrop. The wine list is encyclopedic. Wine-pairing is available for an additional $60 per person (let your server know about any personal wine preferences).

At the end of the meal, guests are given a

souvenir menu and a red rose (ladies only). In sum, though the experience is an extremely expensive one, for many it is also quite special. Jackets are required for men. Guests must be at least 10 years old to dine here. Reservations are necessary.

For an extra-special (and super splurgy) experience, book the Chef's Table (for up to 10 guests) or the new Queen Victoria Room. With just four tables, the latter provides the restaurant's most exclusive, luxurious setting.

POLYNESIAN

Capt. Cook's

B L D S **$-$$**

The Captain dispenses snacks and light fare (both prepared and made to order) 24 hours a day. It's a good spot for breakfast items, burgers, flatbreads, Asian noodle bowls, salads, sushi, sandwiches—including the Adult Grilled Cheese (melted cheddar, Swiss, blue cheese, and tomato on multi-grain sunflower bread), yogurt, fruit, and snacks. Milk (plain and chocolate), beer, wine, and soft drinks are also available. Fans of the Magic Kingdom classic known as Dole Whip, rejoice: the frozen pineapple confection is sold here, too! Come here to buy and fill the Poly's refillable mug.

Kona Cafe

B L D S **$$-$$$**

Warm colors, soft lighting, and South Seas decor render the crisp, fluid design of this dining space cozy and casual. The menu tends toward the exotic side as far as Disney

HOTEL PLAZA BLVD. RESORTS

The properties on Hotel Plaza Boulevard—Best Western Lake Buena Vista, Doubletree Guest Suites, Wyndham Lake Buena Vista, Hilton, Royal Plaza, Buena Vista Palace, and Holiday Inn at Walt Disney World—sit inside WDW boundaries, but are neither owned nor operated by Disney. To make dinner reservations, inquire at the hotel's front desk. Here's the lowdown:

Best Western Lake Buena Vista
Trader's Island Grill serves breakfast and dinner. The **Parakeet Café** offers three meals, plus snacks and to-go items. **Flamingo Cove** serves lunch and cocktails. **Pizza Hut Express** offers pizza (to eat in or take out).

Doubletree by Hilton Guest Suites
A full-service restaurant and pool bar offers a breakfast buffet, lunch, and dinner, plus snacks, sandwiches, and cocktails throughout the day. A market has snacks and groceries.

Wyndham Lake Buena Vista
LakeView Restaurant serves breakfast and dinner daily; Disney characters come for breakfast on Tuesday, Thursday, and Saturday. **Oasis Bar & Grill** is open for lunch and dinner. **Sundial Cafe 24-7**, a store/snack bar located in the lobby, supplies

Continued on page 99

restaurants go, but there's a nice variety of choices. Lunch and dinner menus feature Asian-influenced entrées. Possibilities include teriyaki beef, ginger-crusted rib-eye, market-fresh sustainable fish, and barbecued pork chop. The morning meal offers macadamia pineapple pancakes, steak and eggs, and Tonga toast (banana-stuffed, fried sourdough bread coated with cinnamon sugar), plus traditional breakfast items. There is a solid wine list, and island-inspired cocktails are served. The pressed-pot coffee here is among the best you'll find on Disney property! Reservations are recommended.

 'Ohana

B D **$$$** ♥

'Ohana delivers a classic Disney experience. It's a meticulously themed, family-friendly restaurant, complete with entertainment. An interesting twist of note: 'Ohana's family-style dinner experience—a South Pacific feast prepared in the restaurant's open-fire cooking pit—does not come with a menu, so no decisions need to be made. The oak-grilled skewers of pork and beef just keep coming. Spicy peel-and-eat shrimp, green salad, pineapple-coconut bread, pan-Asian noodles tossed in peanut sauce, and stir-fried veggies are among the accompaniments, and bread pudding served à la mode with warm caramel sauce is served for dessert. Soft drinks are included. Beer, wine, and cocktails are extra.

'Ohana's setting, which features wood carvings under a vast thatched roof, is rather festive. So much so that there are periodic, boisterous hula hoop, limbo, and coconut-rolling contests for the little ones. Polynesian singers croon from time to time.

Breakfast is also a family affair—make

continental breakfast and light fare around the clock. For drinks, there's the **Eclipse Bar**, **Oasis Bar**, and **Horizons Bar**.

Buena Vista Palace Hotel & Spa

The lakeside **Watercress Cafe** serves breakfast and lunch only (Disney characters are in attendance Sunday mornings); the **Watercress Mini Market** is open from 6 A.M. to midnight for baked goods and sandwiches; **Outback Restaurant** (which is not part of the national chain) offers seafood and steak; the **Lobby Lounge** provides a place to sip a glass of fine wine; while armchair quarterbacks enjoy the **Kook Sports Bar**. **Castaway Grill** and **Shipwreck Bar** serve snacks and drinks.

Hilton

Andiamo Italian Bistro & Grille offers American and Italian fare, while **Benihana Steakhouse & Sushi** serves Japanese favorites. Both serve dinner only. **Covington Mill** serves breakfast (with Disney characters in attendance on Sunday) and lunch only. **Rum Largo Poolside Bar & Cafe** offers burgers, sandwiches, salads, and tropical drinks alfresco. **Main Street Market**, open 24 hours, is part deli, part country store.

Continued on page 101

that extended family, as Lilo, Stitch, Mickey, and Pluto host a morning character meal. Breakfast fare is basic and presented family-style. (Platters are shared by the whole party.) Reservations are recommended.

POP CENTURY

 Everything Pop

B L D S $–$$ ☺

The selection at this colorful, modern food court has included pasta, pizza, chicken, roast turkey, Asian dishes, seafood, burgers, hot dogs, sandwiches, salads, pizza, break-fast items, a build-your-own burrito station, and baked goods (tie-dyed cheesecake!). Savory sides include hummus, olive tape-nade, and black bean salad. Feel free to join the cast members as they dance the Twist at 8 A.M. and the Hustle at 6 P.M.

PORT ORLEANS FRENCH QUARTER

Sassagoula Floatworks & Food Factory

B L D S $–$$ ☺

A food court with a Mardi Gras theme, this spot offers pizza, pasta, burgers, sandwiches, soups, salads, spit-roasted chicken, barbe-cued ribs, ice cream, and bakery products. The Big Easy is well represented here; New Orleans-inspired menu items include classic gumbo, Creole burgers, po'boy sandwiches, muffalettas, and jambalaya.

Continued from page 99

For light meals, snacks, or drinks, drop by **John T's Lounge**; specialty coffees and ice cream are served at **Mugs**.

Holiday Inn at Walt Disney World

The newly remodeled hotel has several dining options. The **Palm Breezes Restaurant & Bar** offers three meals a day. It has "grab and go" items, too. **Aqua Luna** is a pleasant, casual poolside spot.

Royal Plaza

The **Giraffe Café** offers three meals a day. Kids ages 10 and under eat breakfast for free with a paying adult. **Sips** serves snacks and sandwiches.

PORT ORLEANS RIVERSIDE

Boatwright's Dining Hall
D **$$–$$$**

Southern specialties and American comfort food are the big draw here—think prime rib and jambalaya. Beer, wine, and cocktails are available, as are soft drinks. The restaurant is quite popular, as it's the resort's only table-service eatery, so reservations are encouraged. Walk-up guests are typically admitted when the restaurant opens at 5 P.M.

🍽 Riverside Mill
B L D S $–$$ 🐭

This food court disguised as a cotton mill (complete with working waterwheel) boasts half a dozen food counters and a sprawling seating area. Expect to find pizza, pasta, fried and grilled chicken, roast turkey, flank steak, burgers, salads, sandwiches (including New Orleans–style muffalettas), baked goods, ice cream, and other snack selections. They're big on "create your own" here, too. (You can design an omelet, salad, and/or pasta dish.) There's ample seating, so it's usually possible to get a table even during the busiest of times. All items may be packaged "to go."

SARATOGA SPRINGS RESORT & SPA

🍽 Artist's Palette
B L D S $–$$ 🐭

Set in a converted artist's loft within Walt Disney World's sprawling resort, this spot offers breakfast, lunch, and dinner. Among the selections are fresh tossed salads, made-to-order sandwiches, pizza, baked goods, and more. There are some grocery items, as well as "grab and go" selections.

🍽 The Turf Club Bar & Grill
L D S $$ 🐭

A restaurant-within-a-lounge with an old-fashioned horse racing theme (and a pool table), this eatery serves burgers, sandwiches, salmon, dry-aged steak, chicken, snacks, and more. Reservations are recommended.

MEALS WiTH CHARACTER(S)

Character meals are the icing on the cake—or, in some cases, the whole cake—for many visitors to Walt's World. As with everything else here, dining with Donald, munching with Mickey, or chatting with Cinderella is the stuff of everlasting memories. Not surprisingly, these events are insanely popular, so be sure to get reservations (see page 10) to avoid disappointment. One other thing to note: The characters scheduled to appear can change at a moment's notice, and if you are expecting Mickey, you may get Minnie or one of their friends. Here's a rundown of the spots that invite you to dine with Disney characters (again, characters and other details may be different when you visit):

Akershus Royal Banquet Hall:
Belle, Jasmine, Snow White, Sleeping Beauty, Mulan, and Ariel (see page 38)

Cape May Cafe:
Goofy, Minnie Mouse, and Donald Duck (see page 111)

Chef Mickey's:
Mickey, Minnie, Goofy, and Donald (see page 87)

Cinderella's Royal Table:
Cinderella and friends (see page 21). Cinderella greets guests in the castle lobby, while her princess friends host meals in the dining room.

Continued on page 104

Continued from page 103

Crystal Palace:
Winnie the Pooh, Tigger, Eeyore, and Piglet (see page 27)

Garden Grill:
Chip and Dale (see page 35). Mickey and Pluto may join the fun.

Garden Grove:
Goofy and Pluto host breakfast here on Saturday and Sunday (see page 105). Timon and Rafiki join them for dinner.

Hollywood & Vine:
Enjoy breakfast and lunch with Disney Junior characters Handy Manny, Special Agent Oso, *Little Einsteins'* June, and Jake the Never Land pirate (see page 56).

Mickey's Backyard Barbecue:
Mickey and his pals appear at this Fort Wilderness dinner show (see page 114).

1900 Park Fare:
Stars like Mary Poppins appear at breakfast. Cinderella and friends (see page 94) are here for dinner. Alice and the Mad Hatter host the Wonderland Tea Party.

'Ohana:
Mickey, Lilo, Stitch, and Pluto (see page 98)

Tusker House:
Donald Duck and friends (see page 67)

SWAN & DOLPHIN

Cabana Bar & Beach Club
L S **$**

Burgers, grilled chicken sandwiches, flat-breads, lump crabmeat salad, fish tacos, and more are offered at this alfresco eatery near the Dolphin's pools. There's a full bar, too.

The Fountain
L D S **$$**

Themed as a sophisticated soda fountain, the Dolphin Fountain is a sleek spot to stop for a meal or a sweet snack. Ice cream is the high-light at The Fountain. Flavors have included dark chocolate, cappuccino, and mint chocolate chip. Burgers, hot dogs, sand-wiches, soups, and salads are also available.

Fresh—Mediterranean Market
B L **$$–$$$**

If you need a quick bite but are looking for more than fast food, Fresh may fit the bill. The menu has included sandwiches, soups, Caesar salads, and entrées with fish, chicken, and pasta. (Some find it a tad on the expen-sive side.) They serve Starbucks coffee, too. You'll find this eatery on the Dolphin resort's first floor, next to The Fountain.

Garden Grove
B L D S **$$–$$$**

This Swan eatery means to transport guests to the peaceful gardens of New York's Central Park—and the 25-foot oak tree is a most realistic touch. The restaurant offers a

RESORT TO RESORT

If you're staying in one resort and dining in another, you need to plan ahead—even if the resorts are linked by monorail or water taxi. Why? The transportation may be operating before dinner, but if you're out late enough you'll have to get yourself home another way.

The good news is you will never be stranded. Bus transportation runs until about 2 A.M.—but it's not direct. If the theme parks are closed, you'll have to take a bus to Downtown Disney and transfer to a bus to your hotel. If the theme parks are open, you can take a bus to any park and transfer to one that's headed to your resort. Keep in mind that the trip can take up to 90 minutes in either direction. If that thought is unpleasant, do what we sometimes do: splurge on a cab. Taxis should run between about $10 and $30, depending on the destination. If you have more than three people in the party, request a van. Ask at your resort's bell services desk.

full breakfast menu (with Disney characters in the house on Saturday and Sunday mornings), and salads, sandwiches, and more for lunch. What's the dinner "special"? It comes with a side of Disney characters! Different nights also bring different fare. At press time, Wednesday and Sunday were featuring barbecue; Saturday, Tuesday, and Thursday offered Mediterranean selections; and Monday and Friday served up seafood.

B *breakfast*   **L** *lunch*   **D** *dinner*   **S** *snacks*

Disney characters are on hand for dinner every night and for breakfast on Saturday and Sunday. Reservations are recommended. Visit *www.swandolphin.com* for details.

📇 Il Mulino New York Trattoria
D $$$–$$$$

A swank Swan destination, Il Mulino offers upscale Italian cuisine in a relaxed yet vibrant bistro-like setting. Specializing in *piatti per il tavolo*, or family-style dining, the spot is ideal for groups. The seasonal menu is characterized by blends of seasonal ingredients drawn from the Abruzzi region of Italy. Signature items include *gamberi al mulino* (jumbo shrimp with spicy dipping sauce), *gnocchi bolognese* (potato dumplings with meat sauce), *pollo fra diavolo* (chicken in a spicy red sauce with sausage), and *salmone* (sautéed salmon in garlic and olive oil with wild mushrooms and broccoli rabe). *Mangia!*

All dinners begin with an antipasti tasting, on the house. Enjoy it while perusing the wine list's 250 or so Italian varietals. The children's menu has pizza, pasta, and chicken parmigiana. For reservations, call 407-939-3463 or 407-934-1199; or visit *www.swandolphin.com*.

📇 Kimonos
D S $$–$$$

In the mood for sushi with a side of karaoke? You've come to the right place! This Swan lounge is an honest-to-goodness karaoke bar (the only one at WDW). Some guests come to sing, while others are drawn by the sushi. This spot opens around dinnertime, serving food and drinks. The singing generally gets started at about 9 P.M. or so. A good time is generally had by all.

⚡ Picabu

B L D S **$$**

A combination cafeteria and convenience store, this Dolphin destination serves sandwiches, salads, burgers, pizza, and more. The merchandise area offers snacks and sundries. It's a bit pricey as fast food goes, but the fare's a cut above average, too. The house coffee is Starbucks. This eatery (and store) stays open 24/7.

🍽 Shula's Steak House

D **$$$$**

Like the original Shula's in Miami, this Dolphin dining spot specializes in generous portions of certified Angus beef, plus chicken and fresh fish dishes. The upscale eatery pays tribute to the 1972 Miami Dolphins—that was the year coach Don Shula led his team to a perfect NFL season. The prices are steep, but the steaks are definitely top-notch and lovingly prepared. Though the interior celebrates the game of football, this is not a casual sports bar. The dress code is business or resort casual. Reservations are recommended. Don't ask for a kids' menu—there isn't one. FYI: The restaurant is a frequent winner of *Wine Spectator*'s Award of Excellence.

⚡ Splash Terrace

L S **$**

A poolside snack bar, this stand serves burgers and other grilled fare, as well as ice cream. Soft drinks, beer, wine, and frozen specialty cocktails are available, too. An assortment of packaged snacks is also on hand.

Todd English's bluezoo

D **$$$–$$$$**

A sophisticated member of the WDW dining scene, the menu at this Dolphin spot features coastal cuisine, incorporating an innovative selection of fresh seafood with both international and New American culinary influences. The raw bar's stocked with juicy (if a little pricey) oysters and middleneck clams. If you prefer your seafood cooked, try the chilled poached jumbo shrimp or chilled Maine lobster tail. A popular starter is the brothy clam chowder with salt-cured bacon and oyster crackers. All of the entrées are tempting: from miso glazed mero to bluezoo's signature dancing fish (roasted on a rotating spit).

Not in the mood for a selection from the sea? Consider dry-aged beef or pan-roasted chicken breast. If you've got room when the dessert menu arrives, expect to be tempted by sweets such as warm chocolate cake with a liquid ganache center. Reservations are recommended. Note that it's possible to get food service at the bar, a plus for small groups or solo diners. Closing time at the bar tends to vary nightly (depending on just how crowded the place is). It's better to get here on the early side.

WILDERNESS LODGE

Artist Point

D **$$$–$$$$** 🔴

The Pacific Northwest theme of this top-notch if under-appreciated restaurant is announced in landscape murals, while tall red-framed windows look out to Bay Lake.

WDW RESORTS

The cavernous dining room is by no means intimate, but it's not without charm.

Artist Point's hallmark is its knack for translating fresh, seasonal ingredients from the Pacific Northwest into flavorful creations. An excellent example is the freshly flown-in salmon served on a smoking cedar plank. The menu may include beef, buffalo, venison, and chicken selections. The wine list features many vintages, including some of the best pinot noirs and syrahs from Oregon and Washington State.

For dessert, many guests swear by the berry cobbler, which is far from the traditional. Ask your server for a description. Reservations are recommended.

Roaring Fork
B L D S $ 🐭

Set in a stone-walled area (a bit dungeon-like, but in a cool way), this snack bar serves salads, burgers, fries, pizza, sandwiches, chili, and snacks. Breakfast items such as cold cereal, yogurt, oatmeal, eggs, and french toast are served. Soft drinks, beer, and wine are also offered. This is also the spot to top off refillable resort mugs. (Purchase the mug and refill it here for free for the length of your stay.)

Whispering Canyon Cafe
B L D $$$ 🐭

The name is ironic, as there is nothing quiet about this place. A family favorite, Whispering Canyon is one of the most boisterous Disney restaurants. All meals are offered à la carte and "all you can eat" style. The latter means heaping plates keep coming to the table until you say "when."

Starting at the crack of dawn, the air is filled with aromas of bacon and hash browns. Lunch offers pulled-pork sandwiches, turkey sandwiches, sautéed quinoa cakes, salads, and more. For supper, expect such items as roast chicken and smoked pork ribs. Reservations are recommended.

YACHT & BEACH CLUB

Beach Club Marketplace
B L D S **$–$$** ♥

The beachy setting extends to this snack bar/convenience store. There are baked goods and packaged "grab and go" items— small salads, sushi, fruit cups, and more. There is limited seating. If you buy a refill-able mug, this is the place to fill 'er up.

Beaches & Cream Soda Shop
L D S **$** ♥

This classic soda fountain is situated pool-side at the Beach Club resort. It serves burgers, chili dogs, and chicken Caesar salads—not to mention ice-cream sundaes, floats, shakes, malts, and sodas. The creamy treats are available to go, too.

Cape May Cafe
B D **$$–$$$** ♥

Goofy and his pals greet Beach Club visitors each morning at this whimsical dining area. The breakfast buffet includes all the stan-dards, plus a few specialties. Breakfast doesn't disappoint, but dinner is the big event here.

Dinner is an all-you-can-eat New England–style clambake buffet, and it's one of WDW's most popular meals and better values. The lineup includes mussels, clams, peel-and-eat shrimp, ribs, corn on the cob, potatoes, salad, and desserts. Soft drinks are included, but cocktails cost extra. Reservations are a must.

🍽️ Captain's Grille
B L D **$$–$$$** 🎃

An airy space (formerly known as Yacht Club Galley) with a subtle nautical theme, this spot serves steaks and seafood (including luscious lobster rolls) for the whole family. Breakfast offerings include a buffet and a full menu; lunch and dinner are à la carte. Reservations are recommended.

🏃 Hurricane Hanna's Grille
L D S **$** 🎃

You can get burgers, salads, hot dogs, sandwiches, ice cream, and soft drinks at this poolside spot. There is a full bar, too.

🍽️ Yachtsman Steakhouse
D **$$$–$$$$** 🎃

You know you're in for a serious steak experience the moment you walk through the door: There's an actual butcher shop here. Yes, Yachtsman delivers an experience to rival those of revered New York steak houses.

The generous portions begin with house-made dinner rolls and may continue with an appetizer, such as lobster bisque. Of course, there's no skimping on the excellent and expertly prepared entrées, so good luck finding room for crème brûlée. The menu also includes chicken and seafood. The dining area is pleasant, with several nooks suited for special occasions. It's a great spot for a big group, too. Reservations are highly recommended.

WDW DINNER SHOWS

At Disney World, the name of the game is entertainment, so why should dinner be any different? In addition to venues where entertainment comes as a complementary side dish (Biergarten in Epcot, Cosmic Ray's in the Magic Kingdom, Sci-Fi Dine-In Theater in Disney's Hollywood Studios, to name just a few), there are three honest-to-goodness dinner shows to choose from. Given their popularity and longevity (the Hoop-Dee-Doo's been packing houses for nearly four decades), there's plenty of reason to plan ahead and book "dinner as event."

Hoop-Dee-Doo Musical Revue (Fort Wilderness) ♥

This family favorite opened in 1974, and it's been going like gangbusters ever since. Every show begins with the stagecoach arrival of a troupe of singers and dancers who proceed to race toward the stage at Fort Wilderness resort's Pioneer Hall. What follows is about 105 minutes of whoopin', hollerin', singing, dancing, and audience participation in a frontier celebration. This being a dinner show, the entertainment comes with unlimited country vittles: ribs, fried chicken (if anything is cold, we request a hot replacement), salad, vegetable, and strawberry shortcake. Soft drinks, wine, and beer are included.

The gags are groaners, but the audience eats 'em up. It's all in the course of an evening at the Hoop-Dee-Doo Musical Revue, presented nightly at 5 P.M., 7:15 P.M., and 9:30 P.M. Cost is about $57 per adult and $30 for children (ages 3 through 9) in Category 3 seating; about $61 for adults and $31 for kids in Category 2; and about $64 for adults and $36 for kids in Category 1. (Category 1 provides the best views of the show.) Prices include tax and gratuity. Reservations are necessary.

The show is presented at Pioneer Hall at Fort Wilderness year-round. Allow yourself plenty of time to get there. The dining room is chilly, especially in the summer. Bring a sweater to combat the air-conditioning.

Mickey's Backyard Barbecue (Fort Wilderness) ♥

It's called a barbecue, but it feels like a country picnic/party, complete with a live band, games for kids, food, and Disney characters.

Presented at an open-air pavilion at Fort Wilderness, the festivities begin with music by a country band. Guests may need little coaxing to get out on the floor to kick up their heels, and Disney characters join the fun.

Dinner consists of barbecue favorites: ribs, chicken, corn on the cob, and baked beans. Beer, wine, and soft drinks are included.

It goes without saying that kids love it, but it appeals to grown-up tastes as well. In fact, many couples appreciate it as an entertaining and unique Disney night out (somehow, line dancing with Goofy has a universal appeal). For big groups, it's a full-out party. The show is presented seasonally. Call 407-939-3463 for a schedule and to purchase tickets. The cost is about $53 per adult and $32 for kids ages 3 to 9. Prices include tax and gratuity. Reservations are recommended.

Hot Tip

Though outdoors, the Spirit of Aloha and Mickey's Backyard BBQ are sheltered and presented rain or shine—but the former may be canceled if the temperature drops below 50 degrees.

Spirit of Aloha (Polynesian Resort) ❤

A decidedly Disney luau show, the Spirit of Aloha invites guests to participate in a "traditional" island musical celebration. Set in the beachfront backyard of a Hawaiian house (at the Polynesian resort), the experience combines traditional music with more contemporary ditties from the Disney film *Lilo and Stitch*. The show, complete with hula skirts, ukuleles, and fire-knife dancers, takes guests on a whirlwind journey from New Zealand to Samoa. It all stems from a (scripted and hokey) premise about a family member who's moved away and lost touch with her roots.

A planned visit from said family member prompts a gathering meant to stir up happy memories of island life.

Presented in an open-air dining theater in Luau Cove, the all-you-can-eat feast is influenced by the flavors of Polynesia. Menu items include roasted chicken, stir-fried rice, and vegetables. The kids' menu features PB&J sandwiches, mac and cheese, and hot dogs. Beer, wine, soft drinks, and dessert are included. Cost is about $56 per adult and $29 for children (ages 3 through 9) in Category 3 seating; $61 for adults and $30 for kids in Category 2; and $66 for adults and $34 for kids in Category 1. (Category 1 provides the best views of the show.) Prices include tax and gratuity and are subject to change. Reservations are necessary.

Plan to arrive about 30 minutes early, and allow extra time for transportation. The show may be canceled due to bad weather.

BOOKING DINNER SHOWS

Dinner shows may be booked up to 180 days ahead by calling 407-WDW-DINE (939-3463). Groups of eight or more should call 407-939-7707.

A credit card number is required for all dinner show reservations. Also, it's very important to remember that cancellations for dinner shows must be made at least 48 hours prior to show-time to avoid paying full price.

To make reservations for Walt Disney World restaurants, dial 407-WDW-DINE (939-3463). The dinner shows are quite popular, so reserve as soon as possible.

WDW Pubs and Lounges

What distinguishes Walt Disney World pubs and lounges from many bars in the real world? Well, in addition to over-the-top theming, you can almost always get a savory nibble to accompany that cocktail. Most WDW lounges serve food, be it from their own menu, or from that of a neighboring restaurant. Hours vary according to venue, but the hot spots at Downtown Disney are usually hopping into the wee hours of the morning.

Theme Parks

ANIMAL KINGDOM

Dawa Bar

A thatched roof provides shade, while the sounds of African music (occasionally live) fill the air. A full bar, including Safari Amber beer, is available. It is beside the Tusker House restaurant in Harambe.

Rainforest Cafe

The colorful Magic Mushroom bar serves, among other things, fruit blends and specialty drinks. Bar stools resemble animal legs (hooves and all). The bar is attached to Rainforest Cafe. Admission to the Animal Kingdom is not necessary to enter. It's possible to order from the restaurant's menu from here, too (see page 65).

EPCOT

Rose & Crown Pub ❤

This watering hole—a veritable symphony of polished woods, brass, and etched glass—adjoins the Rose & Crown Dining Room in the United Kingdom pavilion (see page 48). British, Scottish, and Irish beers are available, along with a score of specialty drinks and appetizing snacks imported from the other side of the Atlantic. On special occasions, there may be live (and lively) piano music.

Sommerfest ♥

Just outside the Biergarten restaurant in Germany (see page 39), there's a shaded spot where soft pretzels, bratwurst, frankfurters, Black Forest cake, and German beer and wine are available.

DISNEY'S HOLLYWOOD STUDIOS

WDW PUBS & LOUNGES

Tune-In Lounge

A sitcom living-room setting, with comfy couches and chairs, characterizes this lounge next to the 50's Prime Time Cafe. Waiters play the roles of sitcom moms and dads, and old TV sets play scenes from beloved sitcoms (all of which feature food). A full bar is available. Appetizers and entrées may be ordered from the attached restaurant (see page 54).

NO PROOF NECESSARY

Soft drinks, fruit juices, and specialty drinks *sans* alcohol are available at all Walt Disney World bars and lounges. Just ask the bartender.

Resorts

ALL-STAR RESORTS

Pool Bars

There are small poolside oases in All-Star Movies, All-Star Music, and All-Star Sports: Silver Screen Spirits, Singing Spirits, and Team Spirits, respectively. Each serves a selection of beer, wine, traditional cocktails, and specialty drinks.

ANIMAL KINGDOM LODGE

Capetown Lounge and Wine Bar

A small lounge area within Jiko—The Cooking Place, this spot offers a selection of African wines and other spirited beverages.

Maji Pool Bar 🐭

A tiny, poolside spot (in Kidani Village), this bar serves cocktails, soft drinks, and snacks until the sun starts to set.

DID YOU KNOW?

At Epcot's Rose & Crown Pub (located in the United Kingdom pavilion at World Showcase) a specially designed ale warmer can heat your Guinness to 55 degrees—the temperature favored by some authentic British pubs.

Sanaa

Located in the resort's Kidani Village, this lounge is adjacent to the restaurant (see page 82) of the same name. South African beers and wines are the specialties of the house.

Uzima Springs

A poolside bar, this small spot serves drinks and snacks during pool hours.

Victoria Falls

A pretty, mezzanine-level lounge overlooking Boma—Flavors of Africa (see page 80) and a waterfall, this bar serves beer and wine with African influences, plus cocktails.

BOARDWALK

Atlantic Dance

This dance hall showcases music (and videos) from the 1970s, '80s, '90s, and today. There's a full bar and a selection of specialty drinks.

Belle Vue Lounge ❦

In the evenings, a full bar accompanies old-time tunes from antique radios in this cozy lounge. Board games are available for on-site use.

Big River Grille & Brewing Works ❦

A working brewpub, this is where patrons may order appetizers at the bar and sample the brewmaster's flagship ales and specialty beers (see page 83).

ESPN Club ❦

The ultimate sports bar provides live broadcasts, along with a menu of ballpark favorites. Occasional trivia contests (with prizes) invite participation by patrons. It's a sports fan's dream come true (see page 83).

Jellyrolls

Dueling pianos and lively sing-alongs are the draw at this club, serving beer and other drinks. There is a cover charge of about $10 (but it can vary). The piano players encourage requests. Don't forget to make the tip jar happy. Guests must be 21 to enter.

Leaping Horse Libations ♥

The poolside bar offers all manner of cocktails—including frozen ones—plus sandwiches in a carnival setting.

CARIBBEAN BEACH

Banana Cabana

Refreshing beverages (cocktails and soft drinks) are served at this poolside bar.

CONTEMPORARY

California Grill Lounge

Prime 15th-story digs afford an eye-level view of the Magic Kingdom fireworks. A selection of California wines, as well as other drinks, plus a full menu, are offered in this tiny space within the California Grill restaurant (see page 86). This lounge seems to shrink more each time we visit, but it's still worth a trip. It opens at about 5 P.M. daily.

DID YOU KNOW?

The Contemporary resort's California Grill serves about 70 pounds of tomatoes *every night* during tomato season (July through November).

Outer Rim

This small lounge overlooking Bay Lake serves all manner of cocktails. It's located on the Grand Concourse level of the resort.

Sand Bar 😊

A full bar is offered poolside, weather permitting. The frozen piña coladas are certainly something to write home about. Fast food in the form of burgers, sandwiches, and salads is available at the adjacent counter area.

The Wave Lounge 😊

On the first floor of the resort, this spacious bar boasts a wine list that is all screw cap (yes, that's a *good* thing)—a quaffable selection of wines from the Southern Hemisphere. About 50 are available by the glass; tasting flights are a great choice for those who wish to sample several selections. Also poured: organic beers, ports, sherries, and specialty drinks. It's possible to order from The Wave's outstanding menu (see page 88). Our humble opinion? The Wave is one of the very best Disney World lounges. It's an excellent place for groups to gather.

CORONADO SPRINGS

Rix Lounge 😊

Located in the resort's main building, this eye- and palate-pleasing lounge serves specialty drinks, beer, wine, and tapas-style appetizers (chorizo flatbread, seafood, and more). Cappuccino is an option. Music may be provided by a deejay or live band.

Siestas 😊

Swimmers can take time out for burgers, sandwiches, tacos, and cocktails at this spot near the pool in the Dig Site area.

FORT WILDERNESS

Crockett's Tavern

Cocktails, beer, and wine are served in a rustic setting. The tavern is inside the Trail's End Restaurant (in Pioneer Hall). Appetizers may be ordered from Trail's End.

GRAND FLORIDIAN

Garden View

A view of the pool and garden area makes this lounge a pleasant place to meet for a drink or dessert. Traditional afternoon tea is also served each day. Reservations are recommended for tea. Note that the tea experience isn't meant to be rushed. Allow time to sip slowly. And come hungry, as you'll be tempted with sandwiches and sweets.

Mizner's

Named after the eccentric architect who defined much of the flavor of southeastern Florida's Gold Coast, this handsome retreat is on the second floor of the main building. Ports, brandies, beer, wine, cocktails, and appetizers are featured. The atmosphere is a bit subdued in the early evening but can be raucous as the hours wear on.

Narcoossee's ☙

This lagoonside bar-within-a-restaurant (see page 94) offers international wines, as well as beer, coffee drinks, and cocktails. It's nice to enjoy a drink on the veranda overlooking the Seven Seas Lagoon.

Pool Bar

A good standby with beer, frozen drinks, and fast-food items.

DISNEY'S OLD KEY WEST

Gurgling Suitcase
This pocket-size lounge on the Turtle Krawl boardwalk serves Key West specialties, along with cocktails, plus beer and wine.

Turtle Shack
Refreshments at this poolside spot include drinks and fast-food selections.

POLYNESIAN

Barefoot Bar
An oasis near the pool, this bar serves beer, frozen drinks, and more. Items of note: frozen strawberry daiquiri and piña colada. (We like 'em mixed, aka the Lava Flow.)

Tambu Lounge
Adjoining 'Ohana restaurant, this small tiki bar offers appetizers and cocktails in a tropical setting. There is a TV, but the view out the window is much more compelling. (Is that a

GOT I.D.?

The legal drinking age in the state of Florida is 21. However, just being 21 isn't enough to get served—you have to prove it. To do so, present a government-issued photo ID. If your driver's license doesn't have a photo, bring it *and* an official photo ID (a passport is ideal). Otherwise, you'll have to stick to soft drinks.

volcano?) The lounge serves as a waiting area for 'Ohana and gets busy during dining hours.

POP CENTURY

Petals
An assortment of specialty drinks, as well as beer, wine, and soft drinks, are available at this colorful pool bar.

PORT ORLEANS FRENCH QUARTER

Mardi Grogs
Beer, specialty drinks, and a small selection of snacks are among the offerings at this poolside spot.

Scat Cat's Club
This New Orleans-style jazz lounge offers specialty drinks, appetizers, and occasional entertainment.

PORT ORLEANS RIVERSIDE

Muddy Rivers
The pool bar serves beer, several specialty concoctions, and salty snacks.

River Roost
Designed as a cotton exchange, this lounge features New Orleans specialty draft beers, plus a full bar and light snacks. There's piano bar-style entertainment Wednesday through Saturday nights, starting at 8:30 P.M.

SWAN & DOLPHIN

Cabana Bar & Beach Club
Beer, frozen drinks, and impressive food selections (crab egg rolls, fish tacos, crab salads, flatbreads, gelato, and more) are the main offerings at this unexpectedly elegant Dolphin poolside spot.

Java Bar
The winding corridors of the Swan lobby have comfortable couches and chairs, punctuated by pianos where musicians often perform. A menu with a variety of specialty coffees and soft drinks is offered daily.

Kimonos
This Swan spot has a full bar and serves sushi and other treats. By night, it's a karaoke/sushi bar. Though big with the convention set, a good time is generally had by all. Come early to get a seat.

Shula's Lounge
This Dolphin watering hole in Shula's Steak House features rich wood tones and comfy seating—the perfect place to sip a cocktail while playing armchair quarterback.

Splash Terrace
Beer, frozen drinks, and fast food are served at this Swan poolside cafe.

WILDERNESS LODGE

Territory Lounge
Located near Artist Point, this homage to explorers of the Old West is a nice spot for a pre-dinner treat. Appetizers, beer, wine, and specialty drinks are served.

Trout Pass

This Wilderness Lodge poolside bar serves beer, wine, and frozen drinks.

YACHT & BEACH CLUB

Ale and Compass ❤

The tiny lobby lounge proffers a full bar and has a nice specialty-drink menu (the Bloody Marys are rather special). They're known for their single-malt scotches, too. A light continental breakfast is served daily.

Crew's Cup

Styled after a traditional New England waterfront pub, this inviting lounge has a seafaring feel to it. It's next door to the Yachtsman Steakhouse, has more than 30 beers, and is a choice spot for a drink. There is an appealing appetizer menu, too.

Hurricane Hanna's Grille ❤

This poolside spot, located near Stormalong Bay between the Yacht Club and Beach Club, offers specialty beverages, frozen drinks, and beer, as well as fast-food items.

Martha's Vineyard

While a full bar is available, wines (by the glass and by the bottle) are the specialties of this house. Appetizers are served.

Hot Tip

Wide World of Sports Cafe is open during select events at the Sports Complex. Call 407-WDW-DINE to see if it will be open during your visit. It is a Disney Dining Plan participant.

Downtown Disney

Bongos Cuban Cafe (West Side)
Housed inside a three-story pineapple is one of the more popular cocktail spots at Walt Disney World. There are booths and bar stools. It's possible to order food from the restaurant menu (see page 70).

Cap'n Jack's Restaurant (Marketplace) ✩
Agleam with copper and right on the water, this bar's specialty is its strawberry margaritas. The garlic oysters and clam chowder on the appetizer menu are great for a snack or a meal (see page 71).

Fuego (Pleasure Island)
Brought to you by Sosa Family Cigars, this small, chic spot features a bar that looks like a melting slab of ice. A full selection of libations is served, as are about 80 cigar brands and cigarettes. This is the only spot at WDW where guests may purchase tobacco products. And, yes, you can smoke here.

House of Blues (West Side)
While there is a traditional bar at the back of the restaurant, it's also possible to have drinks in the enclosed Voodoo Garden (table-service only). Guests may order from the restaurant menu (see page 73).

Raglan Road Irish Pub (Pleasure Island) ✩
Top o' the evenin' to you! This establishment simply oozes Irish charm. Stop in for a pint

and a live music chaser. Guests may sit at tables (and order food) or by the bar. There is no admission charge. *Slainte!* (That's Gaelic for "cheers!")

Shark Bar (T-Rex: A Prehistoric Family Adventure; Marketplace)

Dive into this full-service bar (with an underwater theme) for specialty cocktails such as the T-Rita "cotton tinis." The bar itself resembles a big wave, and, in lieu of the usual tavern TV, patrons have a colorful aquarium to gaze upon while they imbibe or enjoy a selection from the restaurant's surprisingly good menu (see page 76). Though it's a family establishment (the place features a dinosaur theme, after all), Shark Bar is a grown-ups-only watering hole. You must show proper ID to belly up to the bar.

Stone Crab Lounge (Fulton's Crab House, Pleasure Island)

Head to the bow of the ship for one of the best scratch Bloody Marys around. They pair quite nicely with the establishment's oyster bar offerings (see page 72). A full selection of beverages (of both the spirited and virgin varieties) is served at a traditional bar and at tables. Reservations are not required, but guests who wish to snag a table should check in at the podium near the entrance.

Wolfgang Puck Café Bar (West Side)

Okay, it's technically a sushi bar (like that's a bad thing...), but this spot is also a great place to grab a stool and relax with an ice-cold beer. There is a TV (expect to see the local game of the moment) and a simple but savory menu—including selections of the aforementioned sushi (see page 76). It's a good choice when caught without a reservation.

WDW Recipes

Your Disney dining experience doesn't have to end when your vacation does. Though sweet souvenirs molded in the image of the Mouse may prove exceptionally satisfying, there may be more substantial culinary cravings to cure. Though your dining room isn't themed like a drive-in movie theater or a fairy-tale castle, and you rarely entertain princesses or five-foot mice, it's still possible to whip up a little Disney magic in the privacy of your own kitchen. On the pages that follow, we've included some of Walt Disney World's most requested recipes. Just add pixie dust.

Flame Tree BBQ Sauce

Spice up the family barbecue with this fan-favorite from Flame Tree Barbecue at Disney's Animal Kingdom.

1 cup ketchup
¼ cup rice wine vinegar
2 tablespoons molasses
1 tablespoon chili powder
1 tablespoon paprika
1 teaspoon ground turmeric
1 teaspoon ground cumin
½ teaspoon garlic powder
½ teaspoon ground cloves
2 teaspoons onion powder
⅔ cup water
¼ cup packed light brown sugar
1 tablespoon Worcestershire sauce
½ teaspoon salt

Combine all ingredients in a 2-quart saucepan over medium heat. Bring to a simmer, reduce the heat to low, and cook for 25 minutes, stirring frequently.

Use immediately or store in refrigerator for up to two weeks.

Makes 1 cup

Oatmeal Raisin Cookies

Easy and delicious, these crunchy cookies are served at Gasparilla Grill & Games at Disney's Grand Floridian Resort & Spa. This recipe is excerpted from Delicious Disney Desserts.

¾ cup raisins
2 tablespoons rum
1 stick butter, softened
1 teaspoon salt
½ cup sugar
½ cup brown sugar
1 egg
1½ teaspoons molasses
1¼ cups pastry flour
½ cup all-purpose flour
½ teaspoon baking powder
¾ teaspoon baking soda
1 teaspoon cinnamon
¼ cup granola cereal without raisins
¾ cup rolled oats

1. Preheat oven to 350°F. Lightly grease two cookie sheets.
2. In a shallow bowl, soak raisins in rum and set aside.
3. Cream butter, salt, and both sugars with an electric mixer on medium speed. Slowly add the egg and mix thoroughly. Blend in molasses.
4. Add both flours, baking powder, baking soda, cinnamon, granola, oatmeal, and rum-soaked raisins. Mix thoroughly.
5. Drop batter by heaping tablespoons onto cookie sheets, leaving 2 inches between mounds.
6. Bake for 10 to 12 minutes, or until lightly golden brown.

Yields 12 two-ounce, trans-fat-free cookies

Sautéed Shrimp with Feta & Tomato

A favorite starter at the Grand Floridian's Cítricos, this recipe is from Cooking with Mickey and the Disney Chefs.

20 large shrimp, peeled and de-veined
8 plum tomatoes
1 tablespoon extra-virgin olive oil
¼ cup thinly sliced garlic (about 5 large cloves)
1 cup Chardonnay or other dry white wine
¼ cup fresh lemon juice
1 cup diced feta
1 stick butter, cut into pieces and softened
2 tablespoons fresh chopped cilantro
Coarse salt and ground black pepper

WDW RECIPES

1. Cut shrimp in half lengthwise. Remove stem end from tomatoes and cut into large pieces.
2. Heat oil in a large sauté pan over medium-high heat. Add garlic and cook until golden, about 1 minute.
3. Add tomatoes and cook for 2 to 3 minutes, or until softened. Add wine and lemon juice; simmer for 3 to 4 minutes, or until slightly reduced.
4. Reduce heat to medium. Add shrimp and feta, stirring gently to combine, being careful not to break up the feta. Simmer for 3 minutes, or until sauce is thickened slightly and shrimp is cooked through.
5. Add butter and stir gently until melted into sauce. Add cilantro, and salt and pepper to taste. Toss and serve immediately.

Serves 4 to 6

Curry Butternut Soup

Inspired by the diverse flavors of South Africa, this soup is often on the menu at Boma—Flavors of Africa at Disney's Animal Kingdom Lodge (recipe excerpted from the Delicious Disney *cookbook).*

2 tablespoons butter
1 medium onion, chopped
1 clove garlic, chopped
1 teaspoon ground cumin
1 teaspoon ground coriander
Juice of 2 fresh lemons
2 teaspoons Thai red curry paste
    (available in specialty markets)
1 pound butternut squash, peeled, seeded,
    and cut into chunks
2 cups vegetable stock
Coarse salt and freshly ground pepper,
    to taste
2 cups milk
4 tablespoons sour cream
Cilantro for garnish (optional)

1. Melt butter in a large stockpot over medium-high heat. Add onions and garlic and cook about 5 minutes, until tender.
2. Add cumin, coriander, lemon juice, and curry paste.
3. Add squash and vegetable stock. Simmer about 20 minutes, or until squash is easily pierced with a fork.
4. Purée soup in batches until smooth. Add salt and pepper to taste.
5. Return to heat; add milk and sour cream. Do not boil.
6. Adjust the seasoning, if necessary. Garnish with cilantro if desired, and serve immediately.

Serves 6

New England Pot Roast

This all-American dinner favorite is served at Liberty Tree Tavern in Magic Kingdom Park. (The recipe is excerpted from the Delicious Disney *cookbook.)*

¼ cup vegetable oil
Coarse salt, freshly ground pepper
3 pounds boneless beef shoulder roast
1 stick butter (½ cup)
2 cups large diced carrots
2 cups large sliced celery
2 cups large diced onion
¼ cup chopped garlic
2 tablespoons chopped fresh thyme
1 cup all-purpose flour
1 cup Burgundy wine
6 cups beef broth

1. Preheat oven to 350°F.

2. Heat ¼ cup oil in heavy pan, salt and pepper the roast, then brown the meat on all sides. Do not let it scorch.

3. Remove the meat and add butter. After the butter has melted, add carrots, celery, onion, garlic, and fresh thyme. Sauté until vegetables are tender. Stir in the flour, and continue cooking until flour is lightly browned.

4. Stir in burgundy wine and beef broth. Add the meat back into the pan.

5. Cover and bake for 40 minutes to 1 hour, or until meat is fork tender.

Serves 6

Papaya, Avocado, and Grapefruit Salad

Healthy and delicious, this dish is a buffet staple at Boma—Flavors of Africa in Disney's Animal Kingdom Lodge.

1 small papaya
1 ripe but firm avocado
1 grapefruit
10 mint leaves, cut into thin strips
½ cup plain yogurt
2 tablespoons grapefruit juice
1 tablespoon honey

1. Peel the papaya, halve, and scoop out the seeds. Dice into 1-inch cubes.

2. Slice avocado lengthwise all the way around to the pit. Gently twist each side in an opposite direction to separate halves. The pit should remain in one side. Slip a large spoon in between the skin and the meat and scoop out the flesh. Cut into 1-inch cubes.

3. In a large bowl, peel and section the grapefruit, letting the pieces fall into a bowl. (Reserve juice for the dressing.)

4. Add the papaya, avocado, and mint leaves; set aside.

5. In a small bowl, stir together yogurt, grapefruit juice, and honey.

6. Pour the dressing over the fruit and toss gently.

Serves 4 to 6

WDW RECIPES

Guinness Stew

*Rich, hearty Guinness Stew from the Rose &
Crown, is one of the Epcot favorites
featured in the* Delicious Disney *cookbook.*

2 pounds sirloin steak, cut into 1-inch
cubes
½ cup all-purpose flour
2 tablespoons olive oil
2 bay leaves
1 large clove garlic, chopped
1 cup diced yellow onion
½ cup diced carrots
1 tablespoon chopped fresh thyme
1 tablespoon chopped fresh rosemary
¼ teaspoon red chili flakes
1 cup Guinness Stout
Coarse salt, freshly ground pepper, to taste
1 quart beef broth

1. Place steak and flour in a plastic bag; seal
bag, and shake vigorously to coat.
2. Heat oil in a large, heavy-bottomed stock
pot; add steak and cook over medium-high
heat until browned, stirring occasionally.
Reserve remaining flour.
3. Add bay leaves, garlic, onions, and carrots, and cook until tender, about 5 minutes.
Sprinkle in remaining flour; cook 1 minute,
stirring constantly. Add thyme, rosemary,
and chili flakes.
4. Slowly stir in Guinness Stout while scrap-
ing the pan to loosen any particles. Stir until
smooth, thickened, and bubbly. Season with
salt and pepper. Simmer 10 minutes.
5. Slowly stir in beef broth and bring to a
boil. Cover, reduce heat, and simmer 1 hour.
Stew will thicken and reduce by at least a
third. Discard bay leaves before serving.

Serves 6 to 8

Where to Find...

From French fries to filet mignon, fried chicken to seafood cioppino, Disney dishes truly run the gamut. To help you zero in on the eateries that best fit your needs, we've created a handy index of specialized lists. Once you've settled on a particular spot, flip to its entry in the book to learn more about it. And if there's a category you'd like to see but don't—tell us and we'll try to include it in next year's book.

Bakeries/Pastry Shops

Beach Club Marketplace (Beach Club resort)
BoardWalk Bakery (BoardWalk resort)
Boulangerie Patisserie (Epcot, World Showcase)
Kringla Bakeri og Kafe (Epcot, World Showcase)
Kusafiri Coffee Shop & Bakery (Animal Kingdom, Harambe)
Main Street Bakery (Magic Kingdom, Main Street, U.S.A.)
Starring Rolls Cafe (Disney's Hollywood Studios)
Sunshine Seasons (Epcot, The Land)

Barbecue

Flame Tree Barbecue (Animal Kingdom, DinoLand)
Mickey's Backyard Barbecue (see Dinner Shows, page 114)

Best Bang for the Buffet Buck (all-you-can-eat)

Biergarten (Epcot, World Showcase)
Boma—Flavors of Africa (Animal Kingdom Lodge)
Cape May Cafe (Beach Club resort)
Chef Mickey's (Contemporary resort)
Hollywood & Vine (Disney's Hollywood Studios)
1900 Park Fare (Grand Floridian resort)
Trail's End Restaurant (Fort Wilderness resort)
Tusker House (Animal Kingdom, Harambe)

Best with Babies (table-service)

Akershus Royal Banquet Hall (Epcot, World Showcase)
Biergarten (Epcot, World Showcase)
Chef Mickey's (Contemporary resort)
Crystal Palace (Magic Kingdom, Main Street, U.S.A.)
Donald's Safari Breakfast at Tusker House (Animal Kingdom, Harambe)
Garden Grill (Epcot, Future World)
Hollywood & Vine (Disney's Hollywood Studios)
'Ohana (Polynesian resort)
Olivia's Cafe (Disney's Old Key West resort)
Rainforest Cafe (Animal Kingdom and Downtown Disney)
Shutters at Old Port Royale (Caribbean Beach resort)
Tony's Town Square (Magic Kingdom, Main Street, U.S.A.)
Trail's End Restaurant (Fort Wilderness resort)

Brunch
House of Blues (Downtown Disney, West Side)

Buffet (all-you-can-eat)
Akershus Royal Banquet Hall (Epcot, World Showcase
  [appetizers only])
Biergarten (Epcot, World Showcase)
Boma—Flavors of Africa (Animal Kingdom Lodge)
Cape May Cafe (Beach Club resort)
Captain's Grille (breakfast only; Yacht Club resort)
Chef Mickey's (Contemporary resort)
Crystal Palace (Magic Kingdom, Main Street, U.S.A.)
Garden Grove (Swan resort)
Hollywood & Vine (Disney's Hollywood Studios)
1900 Park Fare (Grand Floridian resort)
Trail's End Restaurant (breakfast and dinner; Fort Wilderness)
Tusker House (Animal Kingdom, Harambe)
Wave of American Flavors, The (Contemporary resort,
  breakfast only)

Burgers
Backlot Express (Disney's Hollywood Studios)
Cabana Bar & Grill (Dolphin resort)
Capt. Cook's (Polynesian resort)
Cosmic Ray's Starlight Cafe (Magic Kingdom, Tomorrowland)
Electric Umbrella (Epcot, Future World)
ESPN Club (BoardWalk resort)
Everything Pop (Pop Century resort)
Food Courts (All-Star resorts)
Fountain, The (Dolphin resort)
Liberty Inn (Epcot, World Showcase)
Old Port Royale (Caribbean Beach resort)
Pecos Bill Cafe (Magic Kingdom, Frontierland)
Planet Hollywood (Downtown Disney, West Side)
Restaurantosaurus (Animal Kingdom, DinoLand)
Riverside Mill (Port Orleans Riverside resort)
Sassagoula Floatworks & Food Factory (Port Orleans
  French Quarter resort)
Sci-Fi Dine-In Theater (Disney's Hollywood Studios)
Sunset Ranch Market (Disney's Hollywood Studios)

Cheap Eats—Fast Food

Backlot Express (Disney's Hollywood Studios)
Casey's Corner (Magic Kingdom, Main Street, U.S.A.)
Columbia Harbour House (Magic Kingdom, Liberty Square)
Everything Pop! (Pop Century resort)
Flame Tree Barbecue (Animal Kingdom, DinoLand)
Katsura Grill (Epcot, World Showcase)
Restaurantosaurus (Animal Kingdom, DinoLand)
Sommerfest (Epcot, World Showcase)
Starring Rolls Cafe (Disney's Hollywood Studios)
Sunshine Seasons (Epcot, Future World)
Wolfgang Puck Express (Downtown Disney, Marketplace and West Side)
Yorkshire County Fish Shop (Epcot, World Showcase)

Cheap Eats (relatively speaking)—Table Service

Beaches & Cream Soda Shop (Beach Club resort)
Cape May Cafe (Beach Club resort)
Cap'n Jack's Restaurant (Downtown Disney, Marketplace)
ESPN Club (BoardWalk resort)
Olivia's Cafe (Disney's Old Key West resort)
Planet Hollywood (Downtown Disney, West Side)
Plaza Restaurant (Magic Kingdom, Main Street, U.S.A.)
Rainforest Cafe (Animal Kingdom and Downtown Disney, Marketplace)
Trail's End Restaurant (Fort Wilderness resort)
Tusker House (Animal Kingdom, Harambe)

Disney Characters (dining with)
(see page 103)

Ethnic Eateries
African

Boma—Flavors of Africa (Animal Kingdom Lodge)
Jiko—The Cooking Place (Animal Kingdom Lodge)
Marrakesh (Epcot, World Showcase)
Sanaa (Animal Kingdom Lodge, Kidani Village)
Tangierine Cafe (Epcot, World Showcase)
Tusker House (Animal Kingdom, Harambe)

American

Artist Point (Wilderness Lodge)
Big River Grille & Brewing Works (BoardWalk resort)
Boatwright's Dining Hall (Port Orleans Riverside resort)
California Grill (Contemporary resort)
ESPN Club (BoardWalk resort)
50's Prime Time Cafe (Disney's Hollywood Studios)
Flying Fish Cafe (BoardWalk resort)
Garden Grill (Epcot, Future World)
Grand Floridian Cafe (Grand Floridian resort)
Hollywood Brown Derby (Disney's Hollywood Studios)
House of Blues (Downtown Disney, West Side)
Liberty Inn (Epcot, World Showcase)
Liberty Tree Tavern (Magic Kingdom, Liberty Square)
Narcoossee's (Grand Floridian resort)
1900 Park Fare (Grand Floridian resort)
Olivia's Cafe (Old Key West resort)
Restaurantosaurus (Animal Kingdom, DinoLand)
Sci-Fi Dine-In Theater (Disney's Hollywood Studios)
Trail's End Restaurant (Fort Wilderness resort)
Wave . . . of American Flavors, The (Contemporary resort)

British

Earl of Sandwich (Downtown Disney, Marketplace)
Rose & Crown Pub & Dining Room (Epcot, World Showcase)
Yorkshire County Fish Shop (Epcot, World Showcase)

Canadian

Le Cellier Steakhouse (Epcot, World Showcase)

Chinese and Southeast Asian

Lotus Blossom Cafe (Epcot, World Showcase)
Nine Dragons (Epcot, World Showcase)
Yak & Yeti (Animal Kingdom, Asia)

Cuban

Bongos Cuban Cafe (Downtown Disney, West Side)

French

Bistro de Paris (Epcot, World Showcase)
Boulangerie Patisserie (Epcot, World Showcase)
Chefs de France (Epcot, World Showcase)

German
Biergarten (Epcot, World Showcase)
Sommerfest (Epcot, World Showcase)

Greek/Mediterranean
Kouzzina by Cat Cora (BoardWalk resort)

Italian/Mediterranean
Il Mulino New York Trattoria (Swan resort)
Mama Melrose's Ristorante Italiano (Disney's
   Hollywood Studios)
Pizzafari (Animal Kingdom, Discovery Island)
Portobello (Downtown Disney, Pleasure Island)
Tony's Town Square (Magic Kingdom, Main Street, U.S.A.)
Tutto Italia (Epcot, World Showcase)

Japanese
Katsura Grill (Epcot, World Showcase)
Kimonos (Swan resort)
Teppan Edo (Epcot, World Showcase)
Tokyo Dining (Epcot, World Showcase)

Mexican/Latin American
La Cantina de San Angel (Epcot, World Showcase)
La Hacienda de San Angel (Epcot, World Showcase)
Maya Grill (Coronado Springs resort)
San Angel Inn (Epcot, World Showcase)
Tortuga Tavern (Magic Kingdom, Adventureland)

Norwegian
Akershus Royal Banquet Hall (Epcot, World Showcase)
Kringla Bakeri og Kafe (Epcot, World Showcase)

Family-style (all-you-can-eat)
Akershus Royal Banquet Hall (Epcot, World Showcase)
Garden Grill (Epcot, Future World)
Garden Grove (Swan resort)
Hoop-Dee-Doo Musical Revue (see page 114)
Liberty Tree Tavern (Magic Kingdom, Liberty Square)
Mickey's Backyard Barbecue (see page 114)

'Ohana (Polynesian resort)
Spirit of Aloha (see page 115)
Whispering Canyon Cafe (Wilderness Lodge)

Fruit

Aloha Isle (Magic Kingdom, Adventureland)
Harambe Fruit Market (Animal Kingdom, Harambe)
Liberty Square Market (Magic Kingdom, Liberty Square)
Sunset Ranch Market (Disney's Hollywood Studios)
Sunshine Seasons (Epcot, Future World)

Good for Groups

Biergarten (Epcot, World Showcase)
Boma—Flavors of Africa (Animal Kingdom Lodge)
California Grill (Contemporary resort)
Cape May Cafe (Beach Club resort)
Crystal Palace (Magic Kingdom, Main Street, U.S.A.)
Flame Tree Barbecue (Animal Kingdom, DinoLand)
Flying Fish Cafe (BoardWalk resort)
Hollywood & Vine (Disney's Hollywood Studios)
House of Blues (Downtown Disney, West Side)
Kouzzina by Cat Cora (BoardWalk resort)
Mickey's Backyard Barbecue (see page 114)
Mitsukoshi's Teppan Edo (Epcot, World Showcase)
'Ohana (Polynesian resort)
Raglan Road (Downtown Disney, Pleasure Island)
Sunshine Seasons (Epcot, Future World)
Todd English's bluezoo (Dolphin resort)
Tusker House (Animal Kingdom, Harambe)
Wave . . . of American Flavors, The (Contemporary resort)
Wolfgang Puck Café (Downtown Disney, West Side)
Wolfgang Puck Café—The Dining Room (Downtown
  Disney, West Side)

Hot Dogs

Backlot Express (Disney's Hollywood Studios)
Casey's Corner (Magic Kingdom, Main Street, U.S.A.)
Hurricane Hanna's (Yacht Club resort)
Liberty Inn (Epcot, World Showcase)
Lunching Pad, The (Magic Kingdom, Tomorrowland)
Studio Catering Co. (Disney's Hollywood Studios)

Sunset Ranch Market (Disney's Hollywood Studios)
Wetzel's Pretzels (Downtown Disney, Marketplace and
West Side)

Ice Cream and Frozen Treats

Aloha Isle (Magic Kingdom, Adventureland)
Anandapur Ice Cream Truck (Animal Kingdom, Asia)
Beaches & Cream Soda Shop (Beach Club resort)
Cheshire Cafe (Magic Kingdom, Fantasyland)
Cool Post (Epcot, World Showcase)
Fountain View (Epcot, Future World)
Ghirardelli Ice Cream & Chocolate Shop (Downtown
Disney, Marketplace)
Hollywood Scoops (Disney's Hollywood Studios)
Min & Bill's Dockside Diner (Disney's Hollywood Studios)
Plaza Ice Cream Parlor (Magic Kingdom, Main Street, U.S.A.)
Plaza Restaurant (Magic Kingdom, Main Street, U.S.A.)
Seashore Sweets' (BoardWalk resort)
Storybook Treats (Magic Kingdom, Fantasyland)
Sunshine Tree Terrace (Magic Kingdom, Adventureland)

Kids' Favorites

Akershus Royal Banquet Hall (Epcot, World Showcase)
Cape May Cafe breakfast (Beach Club resort)
Casey's Corner (Magic Kingdom, Main Street, U.S.A.)
Chef Mickey's (Contemporary resort)
Cinderella's Royal Table (Magic Kingdom, Fantasyland)
Crystal Palace (Magic Kingdom, Main Street, U.S.A.)
50's Prime Time Cafe (Disney's Hollywood Studios)
Garden Grill (Epcot, Future World)
Hoop-Dee-Doo Musical Revue (see page 114)
Liberty Inn (Epcot, World Showcase)
1900 Park Fare (Grand Floridian resort)
'Ohana (Polynesian resort)
Pecos Bill Cafe (Magic Kingdom, Frontierland)
Pinocchio Village Haus (Magic Kingdom, Fantasyland)
Pizza Planet (Disney's Hollywood Studios)
Pizzafari (Animal Kingdom, Discovery Island)
Planet Hollywood (Downtown Disney, West Side)
Rainforest Cafe (Animal Kingdom and Downtown Disney,
Marketplace)

Sci-Fi Dine-In Theater (Disney's Hollywood Studios)
Sunset Ranch Market (Disney's Hollywood Studios)
Sunshine Seasons (Epcot, Future World)
T-Rex: A Prehistoric Family Adventure (Downtown Disney,
   Marketplace)
Tusker House (Animal Kingdom, Harambe)
Whispering Canyon Cafe (Wilderness Lodge)

Knockout Views

Big River Grille & Brewing Works (outdoor seating;
   BoardWalk resort)
California Grill (Contemporary resort)
Coral Reef (Epcot, Future World)
La Hacienda de San Angel (Epcot, World Showcase)
Rose & Crown Pub & Dining Room (Epcot, World Showcase)
Sanaa (Animal Kingdom Lodge)
Tomorrowland Terrace (Magic Kingdom, Tomorrowland)

Kosher (fast-food selections)

ABC Commissary (Disney's Hollywood Studios)
Artist's Palette (Saratoga Springs resort)
Cosmic Ray's Starlight Cafe (Magic Kingdom, Tomorrowland)
Everything Pop (Pop Century resort)
Food Courts (All-Star and Port Orleans Riverside resorts)
Gasparilla Grill & Games (Grand Floridian resort)
Liberty Inn (Epcot, World Showcase)
Mara, The (Animal Kingdom Lodge)
Old Port Royale (Caribbean Beach resort)
Pizzafari (Animal Kingdom, Discovery Island)
Roaring Fork (Wilderness Lodge)

Lounges and Bars (with food)

Big River Grille & Brewing Works (BoardWalk resort)
Bongos Cuban Cafe (Downtown Disney, West Side)
Cabana Bar & Grill (Dolphin resort)
California Grill Lounge (Contemporary resort)
Cap'n Jack's Restaurant (Downtown Disney, Marketplace)
Citricos Lounge (Grand Floridian resort)
Crew's Cup (Yacht Club resort)
Crockett's Tavern (Fort Wilderness resort)
ESPN Club (BoardWalk resort)

Garden View (Grand Floridian resort)
Hurricane Hanna's Grille (Yacht & Beach Club resorts)
Il Mulino New York Trattoria Lounge (Swan resort)
Kimonos (Swan resort)
La Cava de Tequila (Epcot, World Showcase)
Leaping Horse Libations (BoardWalk resort)
Mardi Grogs (Port Orleans French Quarter resort)
Martha's Vineyard (Beach Club resort)
Mizner's (Grand Floridian resort)
Muddy Rivers (Port Orleans Riverside resort)
Narcoossee's (Grand Floridian resort)
Outer Rim (Contemporary resort)
Paradiso 37 (Downtown Disney, Pleasure Island)
Portobello (Downtown Disney, Pleasure Island)
Raglan Road (Downtown Disney, Pleasure Island)
Rainforest Cafe (Magic Mushroom bar; Animal Kingdom
   and Downtown Disney, Marketplace)
River Roost (Port Orleans Riverside resort)
Rix Lounge (Coronado Springs resort)
Rose & Crown Pub (Epcot, World Showcase)
Sanaa lounge (Animal Kingdom Lodge)
Sand Bar (Contemporary resort)
Siestas (Coronado Springs resort)
Sommerfest (inside Germany; Epcot, World Showcase)
Splash Terrace (Swan resort)
Stone Crab Lounge (inside Fulton's Crab House;
   Downtown Disney, Pleasure Island)
Tambu Lounge (Polynesian resort)
Territory Lounge (Wilderness Lodge)
Tune-In Lounge (Disney's Hollywood Studios)
Turf Club Bar & Grill, The (Saratoga Springs resort)
Turtle Shack (Disney's Old Key West resort)
Tutto Gusto (Epcot, World Showcase)
Uzima Springs (Animal Kingdom Lodge)
Yak & Yeti Lounge (Disney's Animal Kingdom)

Open 24 Hours
Capt. Cook's (Polynesian resort)
Gasparilla Grill & Games (Grand Floridian resort)
Picabu (Dolphin resort)
Sundial Cafe 24-7 (Wyndham hotel)

Pizza

Capt. Cook's (Polynesian resort)
Everything Pop (Pop Century resort)
Food Courts (All-Star resorts)
Gasparilla Grill & Games (Grand Floridian resort)
Mama Melrose's Ristorante Italiano (Disney's Hollywood
  Studios)
Pinocchio Village Haus (Magic Kingdom, Fantasyland)
Pizza Planet (Disney's Hollywood Studios)
Pizzafari (Animal Kingdom, Discovery Island)
Planet Hollywood (Downtown Disney, West Side)
Riverside Mill (Port Orleans Riverside resort)
Roaring Fork (Wilderness Lodge)
Royale Pizza Shop (Caribbean Beach resort)
Sassagoula Floatworks & Food Factory (Port Orleans
  French Quarter resort)
Sunset Ranch Market (Disney's Hollywood Studios)
Trail's End Restaurant (Fort Wilderness resort)
Via Napoli (Epcot, World Showcase)
Wolfgang Puck Café (Downtown Disney, West Side)
Wolfgang Puck Express (Downtown Disney, Marketplace
  and West Side)

Salads

Artist's Palette (Saratoga Springs resort)
Big River Grille & Brewing Works (BoardWalk resort)
Boma—Flavors of Africa (Animal Kingdom Lodge)
Cape May Cafe (Beach Club resort)
Columbia Harbour House (Magic Kingdom, Liberty Square)
Flame Tree Barbecue (Animal Kingdom, DinoLand)
Hollywood Brown Derby (Disney's Hollywood Studios)
Il Mulino New York Trattoria (Swan resort)
Pecos Bill Cafe (Magic Kingdom, Frontierland)
Pepper Market (Coronado Springs resort)
Pinocchio Village Haus (Magic Kingdom, Fantasyland)
Plaza Restaurant (Magic Kingdom, Main Street, U.S.A.)
Rainforest Cafe (Animal Kingdom and Downtown Disney,
  Marketplace)
Sunshine Seasons (Epcot, Future World)
Wave . . . of American Flavors, The (Contemporary resort)
Wolfgang Puck Café (Downtown Disney, West Side)

Seafood

Artist Point (Wilderness Lodge)
Cape May Cafe (Beach Club resort)
Cap'n Jack's Restaurant (Downtown Disney, Marketplace)
Columbia Harbour House (Magic Kingdom, Liberty Square)
Coral Reef (Epcot, Future World)
Flying Fish Cafe (BoardWalk resort)
Fulton's Crab House (Downtown Disney, Pleasure Island)
Narcoossee's (Grand Floridian resort)
Todd English's bluezoo (Dolphin resort)
Wave . . . of American Flavors, The (Contemporary resort)

Snack Bars (at the resorts)

Beach Club Marketplace (Beach Club resort)
Cabana Bar & Grill (Dolphin resort)
Capt. Cook's (Polynesian resort)
Contempo Café (Contemporary resort)
Gasparilla Grill & Games (Grand Floridian resort)
Mara, The (Animal Kingdom Lodge)
Picabu (Dolphin resort)
Roaring Fork (Wilderness Lodge)
Sand Bar (pool bar; Contemporary resort)

Solo Diners

Cap'n Jack's Restaurant (Downtown Disney, Marketplace)
Citricos lounge (Grand Floridian resort)
Crew's Cup (lounge, Yacht Club resort)
ESPN Club (BoardWalk resort)
Flying Fish Cafe (BoardWalk resort)
Il Mulino New York Trattoria (Swan resort)
Jiko—The Cooking Place lounge (Animal Kingdom Lodge)
Narcoossee's lounge (Grand Floridian resort)
Stone Crab Lounge (inside Fulton's Crab House, Downtown Disney, Pleasure Island)
Tune-In Lounge (Disney's Hollywood Studios)
Wolfgang Puck Café Bar (Downtown Disney, West Side)

Steak

Captain's Grille (Yacht Club resort)
La Hacienda de San Angel (Epcot, World Showcase)

Le Cellier Steakhouse (Epcot, World Showcase)
Shula's Steak House (Dolphin resort)
Yachtsman Steakhouse (Yacht Club resort)

Super Splurges (for grown-ups)

Artist Point (Wilderness Lodge)
Bistro de Paris (Epcot, World Showcase)
California Grill (Contemporary resort)
Chefs de France (Epcot, World Showcase)
Flying Fish Cafe (BoardWalk resort)
Il Mulino (Swan resort)
Jiko—The Cooking Place (Animal Kingdom Lodge)
Le Cellier Steakhouse (Epcot, World Showcase)
Shula's Steak House (Dolphin resort)
Victoria & Albert's (Grand Floridian resort)
Yachtsman Steakhouse (Yacht Club resort)

Sushi

California Grill (Contemporary resort)
Capt. Cook's (Polynesian resort)
Katsura Grill (Epcot, World Showcase)
Kimonos (lounge; Swan resort)
Kona Island (after 5 P.M.; Polynesian resort)
Mitsukoshi's Tokyo Dining (Epcot, World Showcase)
Wolfgang Puck Café (Downtown Disney, West Side)

Terrific Theming

Akershus Royal Banquet Hall (Epcot, World Showcase)
Biergarten (Epcot, World Showcase)
Cinderella's Royal Table (Magic Kingdom, Fantasyland)
50's Prime Time Cafe (Disney's Hollywood Studios)
Liberty Tree Tavern (Magic Kingdom, Liberty Square)
'Ohana (Polynesian resort)
Rainforest Cafe (Animal Kingdom and Downtown Disney, Marketplace)
Sanaa (Animal Kingdom Lodge)
Sci-Fi Dine-In Theater (Disney's Hollywood Studios)
T-Rex: A Prehistoric Family Adventure (Downtown Disney, Marketplace)
Tusker House (Discovery Island, Animal Kingdom)

Vegetarian Selections

Boma—Flavors of Africa (Animal Kingdom Lodge)
Columbia Harbour House (Magic Kingdom, Liberty Square)
Cosmic Ray's Starlight Cafe (Magic Kingdom, Tomorrowland)
Everything Pop (Pop Century resort)
Food Courts (All-Star resorts)
Jiko—The Cooking Place (Animal Kingdom Lodge)
Mama Melrose's Ristorante Italiano (Disney's Hollywood Studios)
Pecos Bill Cafe (Magic Kingdom, Frontierland)
Pizzafari (Animal Kingdom, Discovery Island)
Planet Hollywood (Downtown Disney, West Side)
Rainforest Cafe (Animal Kingdom and Downtown Disney, Marketplace)
Sanaa (Animal Kingdom Lodge)
Sunset Ranch Market (Disney's Hollywood Studios)
Sunshine Seasons (Epcot, Future World)
Tony's Town Square (Magic Kingdom, Main Street, U.S.A.)
Tusker House (Animal Kingdom, Harambe)
Wolfgang Puck Express (Downtown Disney, West Side and Marketplace)

Wine and Dine (great wine lists)

Artist Point (Wilderness Lodge)
Boma—Flavors of Africa (Animal Kingdom Lodge)
California Grill (Contemporary resort)
Chefs de France (Epcot, World Showcase)
Citricos (Grand Floridian resort)
Flying Fish Cafe (BoardWalk resort)
Hollywood Brown Derby (Disney's Hollywood Studios)
Il Mulino New York Trattoria (Swan resort)
Jiko—The Cooking Place (Animal Kingdom Lodge)
Narcoossee's (Grand Floridian resort)
Portobello (Downtown Disney, Pleasure Island)
Sanaa (Animal Kingdom Lodge)
Shula's Steak House (Dolphin resort)
Victoria & Albert's (Grand Floridian resort)
Wave . . . of American Flavors, The (Contemporary resort)
Wolfgang Puck Café—The Dining Room (Downtown Disney, West Side)
Yachtsman Steakhouse (Yacht Club resort)

Index

A

ABC Commissary (Disney's Hollywood Studios), 54, 147
Adventureland, Magic Kingdom, 18
Akershus (World Showcase, Epcot), 38, 144, 146, 151, meals with Disney characters, 103
All-Star resorts (Movies, Music, and Sports), 80
pool bars, 120
Animal Kingdom Lodge, 80–82
pubs and lounges, 120–121
Art of Animation resort, 82
Artist Point (Wilderness Lodge), 16, 78, 109–110, 143, 150–152
Artist's Palette (Saratoga Springs resort), 102, 147, 149
Atlantic Dance (BoardWalk), 121

B

babies, best eateries with (table service), 140
Baby Care Centers, 57–58
Backlot Express (Disney's Hollywood Studios), 54, 141–142, 145
bakeries/pastry shops, 140
Barefoot Bar (Polynesian resort), 125
Beach Club Marketplace (Yacht & Beach Club resorts), 111
Beach Club resort, 79, 111–112
pubs and lounges, 128
Belle Vue Lounge (BoardWalk), 121
Best Western Lake Buena Vista (Hotel Plaza Blvd. resort), 97
Biergarten (World Showcase, Epcot), 39, 113, 140–141, 144–145
Big River Grille & Brewing Works (BoardWalk resort), 12, 78, 83, 121, 143, 147, 149
Bistro de Paris (World Showcase, Epcot), 39–40, 143, 151
Blizzard Beach (water park), 66
BoardWalk resort, 83–85
pubs and lounges, 121–122
Boatwright's Dining Hall (Port Orleans Riverside resort), 101, 143
Boma — Flavors of Africa (Animal Kingdom Lodge), 80–81, 137, 140–142, 145, 149, 152
Bongos Cuban Cafe (West Side, Downtown Disney), 70, 129, 143, 147
breakfast with Disney characters at Cinderella's Royal Table (Fantasyland, Magic Kingdom), 19–22
brunch, 141
Buena Vista Palace (Hotel Plaza Blvd. resort), 58, 97, 99
buffets, all-you-can-eat, 141
family-style, 144–145
burgers, 141
bus transportation between resorts, 106

C

Cabana Bar & Beach Club (Dolphin resort), 105, 127, 141, 147, 150
California Grill (Contemporary resort), 16, 78, 86–87, 143, 145, 147, 151–152
Candlelight Processional (World Showcase, Epcot), 35
Cantina de San Angel, La (World Showcase, Epcot), 43, 144
Cape May Cafe (Beach Club resort), 111–112, 140–141, 149–150
meals with Disney characters, 103
Cap'n Jack's Restaurant (Marketplace, Downtown Disney), 71, 129, 142, 147, 150
Capt. Cook's (Polynesian resort), 96, 141, 148–151
Captain's Grille (Yacht Club), 112, 141, 150
Caribbean Beach resort, 85–86
pubs and lounges, 122
Casey's Corner (Main Street, Magic Kingdom), 26–27, 142, 145–146
Chef Mickey's (Contemporary resort), 87–88, 140–142, 146
meals with Disney characters, 103
Chefs de France (World Showcase, Epcot), 41, 143, 151–152
Cheshire Cafe (Fantasyland, Magic Kingdom), 20, 146
Chinese restaurants, 45–47, 68, 143

Cinderella's Royal Table (Fantasyland, Magic Kingdom), 16, 19–22, 25, 146, 151
    meals with Disney characters, 19–22, 103–104
Cítricos (Grand Floridian resort), 16, 92, 152
Columbia Harbour House (Liberty Square, Magic Kingdom), 24–25, 142, 149–150, 152
confirming dining reservations (dining hotline), 10–12
Contemporary resort, 29, 78, 86–89, 90
    pubs and lounges, 122–123
Coral Reef (Future World, Epcot), 34, 147, 150
Coronado Springs resort, 89–90
    pubs and lounges, 123
Cosmic Ray's Starlight Cafe (Tomorrowland, Magic Kingdom), 32, 113, 141, 147, 152
Crockett's Tavern (Fort Wilderness), 124, 147
Crystal Palace (Main Street, Magic Kingdom), 25, 27–28, 140–141, 145–146
    meals with Disney characters, 104

D

dining gift card. see WDW Shopping and Dining Gift Card
dining plan. see Disney Dining Plan
dinner at sea (Disney Grand 1 yacht), 90
dinner shows, 12, 113–116
    Hoop-Dee-Doo Musical Revue (Fort Wilderness), 12, 16, 113–114, 144, 146
    Mickey's Backyard Barbecue (Fort Wilderness), 114–115, 144–145
    Spirit of Aloha (Polynesian resort), 115–116, 145
Disney characters, meals with, 97, 99, 103–104
Disney Dining Plan, 8, 13–16
Disney Grand 1 yacht (dinner at sea), 90
Disney resort ID, 52
Disney's Animal Kingdom, 63–68
    pubs and lounges, 118

Disney's Hollywood Studios, 53–62
    pubs and lounges, 119
Disney's Old Key West resort, 91
    pubs and lounges, 125
Dolphin resort, 52, 58, 105–109
    pubs and lounges, 127
Donald's Safari Breakfast (Animal Kingdom), 67–68, 140
Doubletree by Hilton Guest Suites (Hotel Plaza Blvd. resort), 97
Downtown Disney. see Marketplace; Pleasure Island; West Side

E

Earl of Sandwich (Marketplace, Downtown Disney), 71–72, 143
Electric Umbrella (Future World, Epcot), 34, 141
Epcot, 33–52
    pubs and lounges, 118–119
    Future World, 34–37
    World Showcase, 38–52
ESPN Club (BoardWalk resort), 12, 83–84, 121, 141–143, 148, 150
ethnic eateries at Walt Disney World, 142–144
    African, 142
    American, 143
    British, 143
    Canadian, 143
    Chinese and Southeast Asian, 143
    Cuban, 143
    French, 143
    German, 144
    Italian/Mediterranean, 144
    Japanese, 144
    Mexican/Latin American, 144
    Norwegian, 144
Everything Pop (Pop Century resort), 100, 141–142, 147, 149, 152

F

Fantasmic! Dining Opportunity Special, 55
Fantasyland, Magic Kingdom, 19–23
50's Prime Time Cafe (Disney's Hollywood Studios), 53, 54–56, 143, 146, 151
Flame Tree Barbecue (Animal Kingdom), 63, 64, 140, 142, 145, 149

Flying Fish Cafe (BoardWalk resort), 16, 78, 84, 143, 150, 152
Food Courts (All-Star and Pop Century resorts), 80, 100, 141, 147, 149, 152
FoodQuest, 70
Fort Wilderness, 91–92
  pubs and lounges, 124
  dinner shows, 114–115
Fresh — Mediterranean Market (Dolphin resort), 78, 105
Frontierland, Magic Kingdom, 23–24
Fulton's Crab House (Pleasure Island, Downtown Disney), 72, 150
Future World, Epcot, 34–37

G

Garden Grill (Future World, Epcot), 35–36, 140, 143–144, 146
  meals with Disney characters, 104
Garden Grove (Swan resort), 78, 105–106, 141, 144
  meals with Disney characters, 104
Garden View (Grand Floridian resort), 93, 124, 148
Gasparilla Grill & Games (Grand Floridian resort), 93, 147–150
Ghirardelli Ice Cream & Chocolate Shop (Marketplace, Downtown Disney), 69, 73, 146
gift cards. see WDW Shopping and Dining Gift Card
Good's Food to Go (Disney's Old Key West resort), 91
Grand Floridian Cafe (Grand Floridian resort), 93–94, 143
Grand Floridian resort, 29, 58, 90, 92–96
  pubs and lounges, 124
group dining, best selection for, 145
Gusto (World Showcase, Epcot), 50

H

Hilton (Hotel Plaza Blvd. resort), 97, 99–101
Holiday Inn, 97, 101
Hollywood & Vine (Disney's Hollywood Studios), 56–58, 140–141, 145

  meals with Disney characters, 104
Hollywood Brown Derby (Disney's Hollywood Studios), 12, 16, 53, 55, 59, 143, 149, 152
Hoop-Dee-Doo Musical Revue (Fort Wilderness), 12, 16, 113–114, 144, 146
hot dogs, 145–146
Hotel Plaza Boulevard resorts, 97–101
House of Blues (West Side, Downtown Disney), 12, 69, 73, 129, 141, 143, 145

I

ice cream/frozen treats, 18, 20, 28–29, 31, 64, 111–112, 146
ID, Disney resort, 52
Il Mulino New York Trattoria (Swan resort), 12, 107, 144, 148–152
International Food and Wine Festival (Epcot), 43
Italian/Mediterranean restaurants, 144

J

Jiko — The Cooking Place (Animal Kingdom Lodge), 16, 78, 81, 142, 151–152

K

Karamel Küche, 40
Katsura Grill (World Showcase, Epcot), 42, 142, 144
kids' favorite restaurants, 146–147
Kimonos (Swan resort), 107, 127, 144, 148, 151
Kona Cafe (Polynesian resort), 78, 96–98
kosher meals, 30, 147
Kouzzina by Cat Cora (BoardWalk resort), 78, 84–85, 144
Kringla Bakeri og Kafe (World Showcase, Epcot), 42, 140, 144
Kusafiri Coffee Shop & Bakery (Animal Kingdom), 65

L

La Cantina de San Angel, 43
La Hacienda de San Angel, 44
lactose-free meals, 30

Landscape of Flavors (Art of Animation resort), 82

Le Cellier Steakhouse (World Showcase, Epcot), 16, 44–45, 151

Liberty Inn (World Showcase, Epcot), 45, 141, 143, 145–147

Liberty Square, Magic Kingdom, 24–26

Liberty Tree Tavern (Liberty Square, Magic Kingdom), 25, 143–144, 151

Lotus Blossom Cafe (World Showcase, Epcot), 45–46, 143

lounges and bars with food, 49, 147–148
See also pubs and lounges

low-sodium meals, 30

Lunching Pad (Tomorrowland, Magic Kingdom), 31–32

M

Magic Kingdom, 17–32
Adventureland, 18
Fantasyland, 19–23
Frontierland, 23–24
Liberty Square, 24–26
Main Street, 26–30
mealtime rush hours, 23
Tomorrowland, 31–32

Main Street, Magic Kingdom, 26–30

Main Street Bakery (Main Street, Magic Kingdom), 28, 140

Main Street Confectionery (Main Street, Magic Kingdom), 26

Mama Melrose's Ristorante Italiano (Disney's Hollywood Studios), 55, 59–60, 144, 149, 152

Mara, The (Animal Kingdom Lodge), 82, 145, 147, 150

Marketplace, Downtown Disney, 69–78
pubs and lounges, 129–130

Marrakesh (World Showcase, Epcot), 46, 142

Martha's Vineyard (Yacht and Beach Club resorts), 128, 148

Maya Grill (Coronado Springs resort), 89, 144

Mickey's Backyard Barbecue (Fort Wilderness), 12, 16, 114–115, 140, 144–145
meals with Disney characters, 104

Min and Bill's Dockside Diner (Disney's Hollywood Studios), 60, 146

Mitsukoshi's Teppan Edo (World Showcase, Epcot), 46–47, 144–145

Mitsukoshi's Tokyo Dining (World Showcase, Epcot), 46–47, 144, 151

N

Narcoossee's (Grand Floridian resort), 16, 94, 124, 143, 147–148, 152

Nine Dragons (World Showcase, Epcot), 47, 143

1900 Park Fare (Grand Floridian resort), 94–95, 140–141, 143, 146
meals with Disney characters, 104

O

'Ohana (Polynesian resort), 98–100, 140, 145–146, 151

Old Port Royale Food Court (Caribbean Beach resort), 85–86, 141, 147

Olivia's Cafe (Disney's Old Key West resort), 91, 140, 142–143

P

Paradiso 37 (Downtown Disney, Pleasure Island), 12, 73–74

pastry shops, 140

Pecos Bill Cafe (Frontierland, Magic Kingdom), 23–24, 141, 146, 149

Pepper Market (Coronado Springs resort), 89–90, 149

Picabu (Dolphin resort), 78, 108, 148, 150

picnics,
in the water parks, 66

Pinocchio Village Haus (Fantasyland, Magic Kingdom), 20–22, 146, 149

pizza, 149

Pizza Planet (Disney's Hollywood Studios), 60, 146, 149

Pizzafari (Disney's Animal

Kingdom), 65, 144, 147, 149, 152

Planet Hollywood (West Side, Downtown Disney), 69, 74, 141–142, 146, 149, 152

Plaza Ice Cream Parlor (Main Street, Magic Kingdom), 28, 146

Plaza Restaurant, The (Main Street, Magic Kingdom), 25, 29, 142, 146, 149

Pleasure Island, Downtown Disney, 69, 72–75

pubs and lounges, 129–130

Polynesian resort, 29, 58, 79, 90 96–100

dinner show, 115–116

pubs and lounges, 125–126

24-hour snack bar, 58

Pop Century resort, 100

pubs and lounges, 126

Port Orleans French Quarter resort, 79, 100

pubs and lounges, 126

Port Orleans Riverside resort, 101–102

pubs and lounges, 126

Portobello (Pleasure Island, Downtown Disney), 12, 74–75, 144, 148, 152

Princess Photo Package, 19, 22

pubs and lounges, 117–130

in Downtown Disney, 129–130

lounges serving food, 147–148

in WDW theme parks, 49, 50, 118–119

in WDW resorts, 120–128

R

Raglan Road (Pleasure Island, Downtown Disney), 12, 75, 129–130, 145, 148

Rainforest Cafe (Animal Kingdom), 65–66, 118, 140, 142, 146, 148, 149, 151–152

Rainforest Cafe (Marketplace, Downtown Disney), 69, 75, 140, 142, 146, 149, 151–152

recipes, 131–138

Restaurantosaurus (Animal Kingdom), 67, 141–143

reservations, 9–12, 21–22, 30, 55, 116

Riverside Mill (Port Orleans Riverside

resort), 102, 141, 149

Rose & Crown Pub and Dining Room (World Showcase, Epcot), 48, 118, 120, 143, 147–148

Royal Anandapur Tea Co. (Animal Kingdom), 67

Royal Plaza Hotel (Hotel Plaza Blvd. resort), 97, 101

S

salads, restaurants featuring, 149

San Angel Inn (World Showcase, Epcot), 48–49, 144

Sanaa, 82, 142, 147–148, 152

Saratoga Springs Resort & Spa, 102

Sassagoula Floatworks & Food Factory (Port Orleans French Quarter resort), 100, 141, 149

Sci-Fi Dine-In Theater (Disney's Hollywood Studios), 61, 113, 141, 143, 147, 151

seafood, 150

shopping gift card. see WDW Shopping and Dining Gift Card

Shula's (Dolphin resort), 108, 151–152

Shutters at Old Port Royale (Caribbean Beach resort), 86, 110

"Signature" restaurants, 16

snack bars, 58, 150

Sommerfest (World Showcase, Epcot), 49–50, 119, 142, 144, 148

special dietary requests, 30

for baby diners, 57–58

kosher foods, 30

refrigerator for your WDW resort room, 87

Spirit of Aloha (Polynesian resort), 12, 16, 115–116, 145

Starring Rolls Cafe (Disney's Hollywood Studios), 62, 140, 142

steak houses, 151–152

Studio Catering Co. (Disney's Hollywood Studios), 62, 145

Sunset Ranch Market (Disney's Hollywood Studios), 62, 141, 146–147, 149, 152

Sunshine Seasons (Future World,

Epcot), 36, 142, 147, 149, 152
sushi, 151
Swan resort, 52, 105–109
pubs and lounges, 127

T

T-Rex: A Prehistoric Family Adventure (Marketplace, Downtown Disney), 69, 76, 147, 151
Tangierine Cafe (World Showcase, Epcot), 50, 142
taxis, 106
tea in the afternoon (Grand Floridian resort), 93
telephone numbers
  to check on restaurant seating availability, 12
  for info on International Food and Wine Festival (Epcot), 43
  reservations for Cinderella's Royal Table, 21
  reservations for dinner shows, 55, 115
  reservations for Fantasmic! Dining Opportunity Special, 55
  for special dietary requests, 30
  WDW dining hotline, 10–12
Todd English's bluezoo (Dolphin resort), 109, 150
Tomorrowland, Magic Kingdom, 31–32
Tomorrowland Terrace (Tomorrowland, Magic Kingdom), 32
Tony's Town Square (Main Street, Magic Kingdom), 25, 29–30, 140, 144, 152
Trail's End Restaurant (Fort Wilderness), 91–92, 140–143, 149
transportation between WDW resorts, 106
traveler's checks, 52
turkey legs, smoked, 31
Tusker House (Animal Kingdom), 63, 67–68, 140–142, 145, 147, 152
Tutto Italia (World Showcase, Epcot), 50–51
24-hour snack bars, 58, 148
Typhoon Lagoon (water park), 66

V

vegetarian meals, 30, 152
Via Napoli (World Showcase, Epcot), 51
Victoria & Albert's (Grand Floridian resort), 95–96, 151–152

W

water parks, 66
water taxi, 29
Wave . . . of American Flavors, The (Contemporary resort), 88–89, 143, 149, 152
WDW Shopping and Dining Gift Card, 37
West Side, Downtown Disney, 69–77
pubs and lounges, 129–130
Wetzel's Pretzels (Marketplace and West Side, Downtown Disney), 76, 146
Whispering Canyon Cafe (Wilderness Lodge), 110–111, 145, 147
Wilderness Lodge, 29, 79, 90, 109–111
pubs and lounges, 127–128
wine (great wine lists), 152
Wolfgang Puck Café (West Side, Downtown Disney), 69, 76–77, 149–151
Wolfgang Puck Café — The Dining Room (West Side, Downtown Disney), 77, 145, 151–152
Wolfgang Puck Express (Marketplace and West Side, Downtown Disney), 77, 142, 149, 152
World Showcase, Epcot, 33, 38–52
www.disneyworld.com, 16

Y

Yacht and Beach Club resorts, 111–112
pubs and lounges, 128
Yachtsman Steakhouse (Yacht Club resort), 12, 16, 112, 151–152
Yak & Yeti (Animal Kingdom), 68, 143